The Need for an Every-Word Bible

A Layman's Guide for Understanding the King James Bible Issue

"For ever, O LORD,
thy word is settled in heaven."

(Psalm 119:89)

The Need for an Every-Word Bible

A Layman's Guide for Understanding the King James Bible Issue

by
Dr. Jack Hyles

September 25, 1926–February 6, 2001

Pastor, First Baptist Church
Hammond, Indiana
1959–2001

Chancellor, Hyles-Anderson College
1972–2001

Superintendent, Hammond Baptist Schools
1970–2001

Superintendent, City Baptist Schools
1978–2001

Dr. Jack Hyles

1st Printing–March 2003
All Scriptures are taken from the King James Bible.

CREDITS:
PROJECT MANAGER: Dr. Bob Marshall
ASSISTANTS: Rochelle Chalifoux, Kristi Wertz
MANUSCRIPT EDITING: Barb Burke, Linda Stubblefield
PAGE DESIGN AND LAYOUT: Arrow Computer Services
PROOFREADING: Elaine Colsten, Linda Flesher,
Martha Gilbert, and Julie Richter
COVER DESIGN: BerylMartin

To order additional books by Dr. Jack Hyles,
contact:
HYLES PUBLICATIONS
523 Sibley Street
Hammond, Indiana 46320

Website: www.hylespublications.com
E-mail: info@hylespublications.com

A Note from Hyles Publications

In an attempt to continue the ministry of our beloved former pastor and leader, Dr. Jack Hyles, we are in the process of assembling materials taught by Brother Hyles from a multitude of sources. No, Brother Hyles did not leave behind dusty manuscripts waiting to be discovered in desk drawers and closets. However, he did leave behind a wealth of materials from his taped sermons available since 1970. He left behind videos of his weekly Saturday night classes where for many years he taught as many as 800 preacher boys. He left behind classic chapel messages he preached at Hyles-Anderson College. He also left behind series of lessons from his Wednesday evening studies. Of course, he left many messages around the nation at churches where he spent a great part of life ministering to others.

Brother Hyles' classic Wednesday evening series on "The King James Bible" was transcribed specifically for this book. Because he is no longer available to read the manuscript compiled for this project, only a minimum amount of editing has been done. Most of that editing was done for clarity, continuity, and to delete some of the repetition in the taped messages that was a classic trait of Brother Hyles.

Much of what Brother Hyles left behind in taped form can

only be shared with others via the printed page. With that thought in mind, please have mercy on us as we work to continue the ministry of Brother Hyles.

Table of Contents

About
Dr. Jack Hyles

JACK HYLES BEGAN preaching at the age of 19 and pastored for over half a century. At the time of his death, First Baptist Church had a membership of over 100,000 with a high year of 20,000 conversions and 10,000 baptisms. For many years the church has been acclaimed to have the "World's Largest Sunday School." During Dr. Hyles' ministry the First Baptist Church's property value increased to over $70,000,000.

In an average week, Dr. Hyles counseled over 150 church members, managed two Christian elementary schools, one Christian junior high school, two Christians high schools, and the largest fundamental Baptist Bible college in America, along with his regular pastoral duties and sermon preparation.

Dr. Hyles left his mark on Christianity, and his legacy remains through the books he wrote, through the sermons he preached, and through the lives he changed. He authored 49 books and pamphlets, exceeding over 10 million copies in sales. He preached over 60,000 sermons; many of his sermons are available on tape.

Dr. Hyles' experience covered numerous evangelistic campaigns, Bible Conferences, etc. He preached in virtually every state of the Union and in many foreign countries. The annual Pastors' School, started by Dr. Hyles, attracts thousands of preachers from every state and many foreign countries.

Lest anyone should be confused with all that Dr. Hyles

accomplished, he did so by spending more than 20 hours a week in prayer and the study of God's Word. He was a firm believer in the surrendered Christian life and the necessity of the Holy Spirit to accomplish much good for God.

Preface

All the Words of God

Proverbs 8:8-9 says, "*All the words of my mouth are in right-eousness; there is nothing froward or perverse in them. They are all plain to him that understandeth, and right to them that find knowledge.*"

I am not going to prove to you in this chapter that the King James Bible is preserved word for word, although I believe it is. I do want to prove to you that somewhere in this world there must be the words of God.

The average statement of faith in the average Baptist church says, "We believe that the Bible is the Word of God in the original manuscripts." There are several problems with this statement.

1. There are no original manuscripts in the world today. There haven't been for many centuries. Suppose someone says that he believes the words are inspired in the original manuscripts. Since we have no originals, then that person must believe in "thought inspiration" or "truth inspiration" and not in the "verbal inspiration" of our Scriptures. If the only place where the words of God are inspired are in the originals, and we have no originals, then we have no words of God unless, in fact, God has preserved His words somewhere.

2. When a preacher says, "In the originals it says…" you

know he doesn't know what he is talking about because he has never seen the originals.

3. We have either "preserved" words or no words. Somewhere in this world, there are words preserved from the time of the originals, or we have no preserved words, because we have no originals.

4. Since the Bible says that its words will be preserved, somewhere in this world there has to be a book that contains the very words of God.

5. When the Bible said that its words were inspired, they had no originals at that time either.

At the top of Psalm chapter 12 it says, "To the chief musician of Shemineth, a Psalm of David." In other words, David wrote this Psalm. David lived approximately 1,000 years before Christ and about 500 years after Moses. The Pentateuch (Genesis through Deuteronomy), written by Moses, was about all the Bible the people had in David's time. David wrote in Psalm 12:6, "*The words of the LORD are pure words.*" Notice the words, *are pure words.* No one can improve on purity. David had no original manuscripts; he did not have the originals of the Pentateuch. Yet, David wrote, "*The words of the LORD are pure....*" He was saying that the every word of the Pentateuch as he had it was pure, even though he did not have an original manuscript.

"*The words of the LORD are pure words: as silver tried in a furnace of earth, purified seven times.*" Seven is God's number of perfection. There are seven colors in the rainbow. There are seven days in a week. There are seven notes in the musical scale. Seven is God's number of perfection and completion. David is saying that the words of God **are** pure 500 years after they were written. Even though the original manuscripts were not available, David said the Word of God was still pure. Psalm 12:7 says, "*Thou shalt keep them, O LORD, thou shalt preserve them from this generation for ever.*" If today is a part of forever,

then His words have been preserved until today. David said
that the words of the oldest written books in the Bible, the
Pentateuch, were at that time pure. David also said that God
would preserve forever those same words as David read them.

It's very scholarly for a Bible college or seminary professor
to say, "Ladies and gentlemen, in the original it says...." He
doesn't have the foggiest idea what it says in the original. Not
one cotton-picking professor has ever seen a copy of the original manuscripts—not one! Even if he is the head of a Bible
department, or has his Ph.D. in Systematic Theology, or is the
best Greek and Hebrew scholar in the world, he has not seen
an original manuscript and cannot truthfully say, "This is what
it says in the original."

So, we must either believe that the words of God are
somewhere today, or we have to believe that God has left us
only the thoughts. If God left us only the thoughts, that means
we can rearrange the words to say the thoughts. Maybe the
Amplified Bible will help us some. Maybe the *Revised Version*
will help us. Maybe the NIV will help us. Maybe the ASV will
help us if all we are asking for is a set of words that convey the
thoughts of God that He has preserved for us.

No! My Bible does not say that God has preserved the
thoughts for us. My Bible does not say that God has preserved
the doctrine for us. My Bible does not say that God has preserved certain truths for us. My Bible says that the words of
God are perfectly pure and will be preserved forever! Since
today is a part of forever, that means somewhere in this world
there must be the very words of God.

The Bible calls itself several things: sometimes the Bible is
called *"the commandments of the Lord,"* sometimes *"the statutes
of the Lord,"* sometimes *"the law of the Lord."* There are different words for the Bible. In reading Psalm 119, numbers of different words are used that mean "the Bible."

In Psalm 19:7 David wrote, *"The law of the LORD is per-*

fect...." He was saying that at that very moment Genesis, Exodus, Leviticus, Numbers, and Deuteronomy were perfect. The verse continues, *"...converting the soul: the testimony of the LORD is sure, making wise the simple. The statutes of the LORD are right, rejoicing the heart: the commandment of the LORD is pure, enlightening the eyes. The fear of the LORD is clean, enduring for ever: the judgments of the LORD are true and righteous altogether."* (Psalm 19:7-9) In these verses, the Word of God is called *"perfect,"* *"right,"* *"clean,"* *"true,"* and *"righteous."* Though he had no original manuscripts, David says that at that moment the words of God were perfect, right, clean, true, and righteous. God had to preserve the very words of the Pentateuch for 500 years for David to have the perfect words of God.

Proverbs 8:8 says, *"All the words of my mouth are in righteousness...."* Suppose the *American Standard Version* contains the very words of God. Then is the King James Bible right? No. Suppose the NIV has the very words of God. Then if the NIV has the very words of God, then does the ASV contain the very words of God if they are not the exact same words as the NIV? No. If God has preserved His words, then only one set of words can be the preserved ones.

Please put aside your prejudice, your preconceived concepts, your denominational background, and your pride. Is there or is there not a place where one can find the preserved words of God Almighty? Proverbs 8:8 says, *"All the words of my mouth are in righteousness; there is nothing froward* [crooked] *or perverse* [hard to understand] *in them."* Wherever God's Book is, this verse says the words are easy to understand. His words are not crooked nor hard to understand. I promise, an eighth-grade student can read the King James Bible and understand it if he will pay attention to it; especially if that eighth-grade student has the Author living inside him. When a person gets saved, the Holy Spirit comes in. The Holy Spirit can teach you His Book. He will tell you what it says while you read it.

Proverbs 8:9 says, "*They are all plain to him that understandeth, and right to them that find knowledge.*" Proverbs 30:5 says, "*Every word of God is pure....*" What more do you want! How much plainer can it be? This verse was written 500 to 600 years after Moses. Solomon, who was the wisest man in all the world, said that every word of God "is pure" at that time.

Proverbs 30:6 says, "*Add thou not unto his words....*" Solomon said not to add anything to the word of God. He said, "Do not add anything to the book of Genesis. Do not add anything to Exodus. Do not you add anything to Leviticus or Numbers or Deuteronomy." Solomon said that at that time every word of God that he had was pure.

In Luke 24:27, Jesus is talking and says, "*And beginning at Moses and all the prophets, he expounded unto them in all the scriptures the things concerning himself.*" He continues in verse 44, "*...These are the words which I spake unto you, while I was yet with you, that all things must be fulfilled, which were written in the law of Moses, and in the prophets, and in the psalms, concerning me.*" David said, "Don't add anything to the Pentateuch." Jesus said, "All the words are true in the Pentateuch, in the Psalms, and the prophets."

In the last book of the Bible, Revelation 22:18, 19 says that we are not to add or subtract anything from any part of the Bible. The law of Moses was written 1,500 years before Jesus spoke in Luke 24. The Psalms were written 1,000 years before Jesus spoke. The prophets were written an average of 700 years before Jesus said this, and there were no original manuscripts.

You say, "Brother Hyles, they found the originals in the Dead Sea Scrolls." No, they did not! Nobody has any manuscript even near the originals. Either somewhere in this world there is a book that contains the words of God that God has preserved word for word, or Christians have to believe in thought inspiration. The Bible does not say that every thought is preserved, every truth is pure, and every doctrine is pure. No! The Bible says, "*every word*" is preserved.

At this point, I'm not trying to convince anyone that the King James Bible contains the very words of God. I am trying to get you to accept that there is **one**. You cannot believe that all Bibles contain the words of God. Only one can be right because the words are not the same in all these so-called Bibles. Use your head! If God's words are preserved, they are written down somewhere. If two books do not contain the same words, one of them cannot contain the words of God.

If we do not have the words of God, we cannot obey the commandments of God concerning those words. Deuteronomy 4:10 says, "*...make them* [my people] *hear my words....*" If we don't have the words, we can't make the people hear the words.

Deuteronomy 17:19 says, "*...keep all the words of this law and these statutes, to do them.*" If we don't have all the words, we can't keep them.

Deuteronomy 29:29 says, "*...do all the words....*" A child could figure out that in order to "do all the words," he must have all the words. Even a seminary professor should be able to figure that out after a few years!

Deuteronomy 31:12 says, "*...observe to do all the words of this law.*" Deuteronomy 32:46a says, "*...set your hearts unto all the words....*" Deuteronomy 32:46 also says, "*...command your children to observe to do, all the words of this law.*" If God commands us to teach our children the very words of God and we don't have the very words, then we can't teach them to our children. He didn't say to teach our children the thoughts; He said to teach the very words of God to our children. How can we teach the words of God if we do not have the words of God?

Matthew 4:4 says, "*... Man shall not live by bread alone, but by every word that proceedeth out of the mouth of God.*" The Bible says, "*every word,*" not every thought, not every truth, but "*every word!*" You cannot live if you don't have "*every word.*"

John 15:7 says, "*If ye abide in me, and my words abide in you, ye shall ask what ye will, and it shall be done unto you.*" The Bible says, "*my words,*" not "my thoughts" or "my truths" or "my doctrine." No! It says, "*my words.*" If the words of God must abide in you so that you can get your prayers answered, then the words of God must be somewhere. Would Jesus have told us to do something that was impossible to do?

In David's time there were no originals, but **the Bible was pure.** In Solomon's time there were no originals, but **the Bible was pure.** In Jesus' time there were no originals, but **the Bible was pure.** So, we know that God preserved His words from David's time and Solomon's time until the prophets' time because Jesus said that God did. Again, we know that God's words were preserved until the time of Jesus because that was a part of forever just as today is also a part of forever.

If you have to have all of the words of God to live and to get your prayers answered and to teach your children, I would start my search if I were you.

Chapter One

The Need for
an Every-Word Bible

Without anybody's book or without any enlightenment, let's study the subject of the preservation of God's Word from the logic of the common man. Let's logically try to arrive at where the words of God are, if, in fact, they do exist.

Luke 21:33 says, *"Heaven and earth shall pass away: but my words shall not pass away."* This verse means that the words of God are in existence today.

Isaiah 40:8 says, *"The grass withereth, the flower fadeth: but the word of our God shall stand for ever."*

Psalm 19:7-9 states, *"The law of the LORD is perfect, converting the soul: the testimony of the LORD is sure, making wise the simple. The statutes of the LORD are right, rejoicing the heart: the commandment of the LORD is pure, enlightening the eyes. The fear of the LORD is clean, enduring for ever: the judgments of the LORD are true and righteous altogether."*

These verses, which were written hundreds of years after the law was given, mean that God has preserved His words. Notice the words, *"is pure,"* from Psalm 19:8. This verse did not say, "was pure in the original."

I ask myself these questions as I search for an answer as a common man and not as a theologian:

- Could somebody tell me where the Bible is?

- Where is that perfect Book?
- Where is that Book that contains the very words of God?

We have heard all of our lives about the inspired Word of God. We have heard preachers say, "I'm going to preach the Word." Where are those pure words of God? Where is that Book?

First, don't tell me where it is; tell me that it exists. If you can convince me that it exists, I am going to find it. If it is somewhere in the Middle East beneath the earth, I am going to go find it. For you see, I must have that Book.

Where Is This Perfect Book?

Where is that Book that contains the pure, preserved words of Almighty God? It's important! I must have it to be saved. Ephesians 2:8 says, *"For by grace are ye saved through faith...."*

How then can I get that faith? Romans 10:17 says, *"So then faith cometh by hearing, and hearing by the word of God."* So, without this perfect Book, I cannot have faith because " ... *faith cometh by hearing, and hearing by the word of God."* Where is this perfect Book? Where is this Book with words that are pure, preserved by God Himself?

I Peter 1:23 says, *"Being born again, not of corruptible seed, but of incorruptible, by the word of God...."* That means I have to find an incorruptible Word of God somewhere. I've got to find the pure words of God, or I cannot be saved.

Where Is This Perfect Book?

I must have it to go soul winning. Psalm 126:6 says, *"He that goeth forth and weepeth, bearing precious seed...."* I have to have that precious seed. I cannot have a diluted seed, an imperfect seed. I have to have a precious seed. And if I go soul winning, I must bear that seed. It may be that I read it, or it may be that I quote it. I do not necessarily have to have it in my hands in printed form, but I've got to have this Book somewhere. Somebody, tell me where is this perfect Book?

Where Is This Perfect Book?

I must have it to live as a Christian and to grow as a child of God. Matthew 4:4 says, "...*Man shall not live by bread alone, but by every word that proceedeth out of the mouth of God.*" That means that as a child of God, I cannot live the Christian life without the Word of God. I've got to find this perfect Book. I must find this perfect Book that is without error with every word of God preserved.

Where Is This Perfect Book?

I must have it to get my prayers answered. John 15:7 says, "*If ye abide in me, and my words abide in you....*" I must have this Book.

Where Is This Perfect Book?

I must have it to know the will of God. Psalm 119:105 says, "*Thy word is a lamp unto my feet, and a light unto my path.*" I need this Book to find the will of God. Somebody, tell me. Where is this perfect book?

Where Is This Perfect Book?

I must have it to fight the Devil. Ephesians 6:17 says, "...*the sword of the Spirit, which is the word of God.*" I cannot fight the Devil without this Book.

Where Is This Perfect Book?

In II Timothy 4:2, I'm commanded to preach it. If I don't have it, how can I preach it? Would God call a man to preach His Word and not give it to him? Would God call a man and say, "I'm calling you to spend your life, full-time, preaching the Gospel. Preach the Word!" and not give him a copy of the Word? I would step down from behind the pulpit and never walk in it again to preach if I didn't have the Word of God in my hands. I would not waste my church members' time or take their money unless I could say to them that they have the Word of God, and I have it to preach. I just don't believe God would give a divine call to a man to preach God's Word and when the man asks God, "Where are Your words?" God would answer, "We don't have them anymore." Looks like anybody would agree that if God gave us the command to preach the Word, then God would give us the Word to preach. That's logic. I've got to have it. Tell me, somebody, where is the Bible?

Where Is This Perfect Book?

I must have it to give to all the world. Would God say, "*Go into all the world and preach the Gospel*," and not give us His Word to take with us? I don't believe that God would send young men to the mission field halfway around the world, to proclaim God's Word without giving him a copy of it.

Of all the nations on the face of this earth, America is the center of world evangelization. America is the only hope for the world, Gospel-wise. Do you think that God would not give His Word to America? The countries of this world look to America for missionaries. These countries look to America for preachers. Every great movement of God in the world today was founded by a ministry or a movement that was propelled by American evangelization and the mission movement, founded basically, I think, by Hudson Taylor. Of all the nations on the face of this earth, it seems to me that God would give the key nation the Word of God.

I know this perfect Book is somewhere in the world because Psalm 12:7 tells me that God has preserved His Word for all generations. So, I know it has to be somewhere. There is such a Book somewhere. There is a perfect Book preserved for me because God said that He would preserve His Word for-ever unto all generations. So I have to find it.

There are two possible sources. One must be true, and the other must be false. Two things that don't agree cannot both be right. If one book says, "2+2=4," and one book says, "2+2 =5," one book is right; and one book is wrong. Both books cannot be right.

Satan has a counterfeit for all that God has. God has a plan of salvation: by grace through faith. Satan has a plan of salvation: by works. God has a plan of salvation which says to trust what God has done. Satan has a plan of salvation which says to trust what man does. Not only does Satan have a coun-terfeit plan of salvation, he also has a counterfeit baptism. God has a plan for baptism: by immersion in water. Satan has a bap-tism: by sprinkling. God has the Lord's Supper. Satan has a counterfeit. He calls it sacraments. For everything that God has, Satan has a counterfeit. God has a church. Jesus said in Matthew 16:18, "...upon this rock I will build my church...." Satan has a counterfeit: the invisible universal church. There is no such thing as the invisible, universal church.

Since Satan has a counterfeit for everything that God has, logic tells me that something so important as the Word of God would also be counterfeited by the Devil. I ask you, where is that perfect Book? It must be **one** of the following:

1. That perfect Book must be perfect only in the original autographs or manuscripts; the only words of God are the words they had back when the originals were written. If this is true, then I have no perfect Bible.

A well-known Christian university professor stated the following concerning I John 5:7: "Thus, according to John's account, there are three that bear record in Heaven. The rest of verse seven and the first nine words of verse eight are not in the original and are not to be considered as part of the Word of God." I'd like to ask that professor a question. "When did you see the originals?" How does he know these words are not in the originals? The only way an honest man could say that these words are not in the originals is if he had seen the originals; however, the originals are not available.

In the *Scofield Reference Bible*, we read that Mr. Scofield says about I John 5:7, "It is generally agreed that verse seven has no real authority and has been inserted." I'd like to ask Mr. Scofield when he saw the originals? He never saw them. He sat in somebody's Bible class, and some Dr. Mess-em-up or Dr. McFuddle stood up and said, "In the original manuscripts...." That sounds scholarly, but nobody in our generation has seen the originals.

If it be true that the only words of God are in the originals, then I have no Bible to preach. I have no Bible to take soul winning. I have no Bible to get my prayers answered. I have no Bible to know the will of God for my life. I have no Bible to grow in the grace and knowledge of our Lord and Saviour Jesus Christ.

2. The perfect words of God must be somewhere in a Book.

3. The perfect words of God are in a combination of Books.

There are only two sources from which we even can claim that either must be the Words of God. The first choice: In 1516, a man named Erasmus compiled, edited, and printed what is called the *Textus Receptus*. That *Textus Receptus* is the source of the King James Bible. The *Textus Receptus* is what we would call the manuscripts for the Protestants, the Baptists, and all other non-Catholics.

The second choice is the *Alexandrian manuscripts*. These are the manuscripts from which the Westcott and Hort came. These are also the manuscripts from which come the other versions of the Bible such as the *American Standard Version*, the *New American Standard Version,* the *Revised Standard Version,* and the *New International Version.* The *Alexandrian manuscripts* are composed of several different sections, but one is called the *Vatican manuscripts.* These manuscripts were hidden for centuries in the Catholic church. From these manuscripts came the *Catholic Bible* along with its Apocrypha. The *Alexandrian manuscripts* are the Catholic manuscripts.

I have only two choices: the *Catholic Bible* kept in the Catholic church or the King James Bible which has been used in every great revival by every great soul-winning church and by every great pastor in history. These are my only choices.

Somebody tell me, where is this Book? Where is the Bible? I know there must be one because God said that it would be preserved. I have a choice. Am I going to take the *Textus Receptus* which has been the Baptist and Protestant Bible through the years, or am I going to take the one that has been hidden in Roman Catholicism—the *Vatican Manuscripts* and the *Alexandrian manuscripts?* I must conclude, the *Textus Receptus* are the preserved manuscripts.

The chairman of the Bible Department at a well-known Bible college said, "I defend every word of the original autographs of the Greek and Hebrew text of the Bible. The Greek and Hebrew manuscripts which agree most closely with the autographs ought to be followed. They are known as the Alexandrian text."

The Alexandrian Texts are the ones preserved in the Catholic church. They are the ones from which came the *New American Standard Version,* which takes away the deity of Christ, the worship of Christ, and the plan of salvation. The NASV leaves out words by the hundreds. "Mr. Chairman of the Bible Department" is saying that the *New American Standard Version* is nearer the words of God than the King James Bible.

He continued, "Every good commentary on the Bible

attempts to bring out the correct meaning of the texts and remove any misconceptions that the English versions might cause. The King James Bible is a good English translation. I've used it all my life and highly recommend it. There is no perfect English translation." This statement is from the chairman of Bible at one of our well-known Bible colleges. He said, "There is no perfect translation." He is full of prunes! What am I going to preach? What am I going to take soul winning? If there is no perfect English translation, I have no perfect Bible. My mother was wrong, and so was yours.

"Mr. Chairman of the Bible Department" continued, "The original Greek and Hebrew manuscripts are the inerrant Word of God. Every English translation and every commentary have personal interpretations in them. The *New American Standard Bible and Testament* is a vibrant and living translation." [That's the one that leaves out the word *begotten* and *firstborn son*.] "It is a beautiful blend of precision, vitality, and reverence. Its accuracy and faithfulness to the Greek text is phenomenal. After comparing it, word for word, with the Greek text as well as with a dozen representative modern translations, I am convinced that it is the finest modern language translation that has yet appeared."

Don't tell me I've been preaching from an imperfect Bible for 50 years! Don't tell me First Baptist Church of Hammond is built on an imperfect Bible! Don't be loyal to some institution! Be loyal to God's Book.

So, this Bible Department chairman is telling me to choose the *Alexandrian Text* of the Catholic church. Do you get it? He's saying you do not have a Bible. I would have more respect for him if he had said that the *New American Standard Version* is perfect. At least he would have said he had a perfect Bible. Notice his title: "Chairman of Division of Bible." He doesn't even have a Bible! Perhaps that title "Division of Bible" means he has divided the Bible.

Mr. Chairman continues, "Every believer should study his Bible with faith and should ask God to preserve him from error." That statement means that every believer can be more perfect than the Word of God. That means you are studying an imperfect Bible, asking God to tell you when you get to something that is imperfect. His title should be "Chairman of the No Bible Department."

If the day ever comes that some teacher at Hyles-Anderson College teaches that we have no perfect English translation in the King James Bible, that rascal will never walk on campus again. He'll never teach another class. If I'm not alive, I'll grab that lever in Heaven that turns on hurricanes and tornadoes and send them to Hyles-Anderson College to destroy the whole campus.

If we have no perfect English Bible, what am I going to preach? What seed am I going to take soul winning? How am I going to live? I have to live by every word. How am I going to get my prayers answered? How can I find the will of God? How can I live a life for Christ when I have to have every word by which to live?

How Will I Choose?

- **I'll choose by association.** The Pope has one Bible (from the *Alexandrian manuscripts*), and D. L. Moody has another Bible, the King James Bible. It's not hard for me to decide. Norman Vincent Peale has the *Alexandrian text*, and Billy Sunday had the *Textus Receptus*. It's not hard for me to decide. Robert Schuller has the *Alexandrian text*, and Charles Spurgeon had the King James Bible. You can have your Schuller, I'll take Spurgeon. You can have your Pope; I'll take Moody. You can have your Norman Vincent Peale; I'll take Billy Sunday. Take all your liberals! Take the National Council of Churches that put out the *Revised Standard Version*! Take them all—they all came from the *Alexandrian text*. You give me the Bible of my mama and of great men of God like Dwight L. Moody, Billy Sunday, Charles Spurgeon, J. Frank Norris, Lester Roloff, Dr. Tom Malone, Dr. Bob Gray, Dr. Harold Sightler, Dr. Oliver B. Greene, and Dr. Wally Beebe; and you can have your *Alexandrian text*.

How Will I Choose?

• **I'll choose by motive.** The *Revised Standard Version* which came from the *Alexandrian text* was copyrighted in 1952 by the National Council of Churches. The *New American Standard Version* was copyrighted in 1977 by the Lockman Foundation. The *Living Bible* was copyrighted in 1971 by the Tyndale House Publishers. The *Good News Bible* was copyrighted in 1976 by the American Bible Society. The NIV was copyrighted in 1973 by the New York Bible Society. The word *copyright* means "the legal protection given to authors and artists to prevent the reproduction of their work." Now those rascals are saying they are the authors of the Bible. I agree with them; it is their work. The King James Bible is God's work, and the other Bibles are the work of the Bible publishers. God is the Author of the King James Bible, and men are the authors of the other books.

I was preaching at a bus convention and afterward signing Bibles. A man handed me a so-called Bible to sign. I said, "I can't sign this; it's not a Bible. I sign only Bibles."

He said, "It says on the outside 'Holy Bible.'"

I said, "Yes, it's full of holes on the inside. That's a *New American Standard Version*. I'm not going to sign that. Now I'm sure that nobody ever taught you any differently and I'm sure that you're a new Christian and as innocent as can be."

He said in a kidding way, "Will you sign my song book?"

I said, "Yes, I will, but I won't sign a NASV."

The last night of the convention as I was signing some Bibles, a man handed me his Bible and said, "Would you sign my Bible?" It was the same fellow with a big grin on his face. He said, "I went out this afternoon and bought me a King James Bible." I signed it.

How Will I Choose?

- **I'll choose the one that has worked.** I'll choose the one over which widows have wept and prayed for their children. I'll choose the one that dear mothers in the history of our country read, loved, and taught. I'll choose the one for which faithful evangelists have given their lives and the ones for which missionaries have circled the globe. I'll choose the one that has caused people to leave their home, family, and friends to carry its message. I'll choose the one that has changed lives and has changed a nation. I'll choose the one Mr. Moody used and the one Mr. Sunday used. I'll choose the one great soul-winning churches in America have used.

I'll choose the one that Mr. Hitler said he would destroy but couldn't. I'll choose the one that Thomas Paine spoke of when he said that within one generation the Bible would not be printed anymore. Yet, after his death, and on the same printing press that his garbage was printed, more Bibles were printed. I'll choose the one that couldn't be destroyed. The Bible says in Luke 21:33, "...*my word shall not pass away.*" I'll choose the one that has stood the test of time.

For which candidate for Bible am I going to vote? I'm not going to vote for the Catholic candidate. I'm going to vote for the Protestant, Baptist candidate. I'm not going to vote for the one that was locked up in the Vatican for hundreds of years. I'm going to vote for the one that has been used by God's people for hundreds of years. I'm going to vote for the one that has been proved and tested.

I must have a Bible because God told me to preach it. I must have a Bible because God told me that I have to live by it. I have to have a Bible to show me the will of God. I have to have a Bible to use in soul winning. I have to have a Bible to save my soul. I must have it!

Remember; if one Bible is true, the other Bible must be false. If one is genuine, the other is counterfeit.

Here are some other examples: Dr. Wilbur Smith said, "In my opinion, this [the *New American Standard Version*] is certainly the most accurate and most revealing translation of the New Testament we now have. I intend to keep it on my desk for immediate access during the years that remain to me."

Dr. William Culbertson said, "Actually, more than a revision, the *New American Standard Bible* is a good translation in contemporary English, and it will be a great help to serious students of the Bible."

Dr. Merrill Tinley said, "My personal feeling is that as a translation [the NASV], it is about the best I've seen for study purposes, since it is sufficiently up to date to be comprehensible. At the same time, it is sufficiently literal to carry the underlying sense of the text. It is, of course, a translation and not a linguistic commentary."

You say, "If the *Alexandrian text* came from the Catholic churches, then why do these non-denomationalists approve of the Bibles from the *Alexandrian text*? They approve because they too came from the Catholic church as did the Methodists and the Presbyterians. Baptists did not come from the Catholic church.

The non-denominational movement in America is deadly and very "encompassing" to the false bibles and liberal teaching. It is the nesting place of the so-called invisible church, for the hatching of new Bibles, and the *Alexandrian Text*. Can't you hear these liberal professors getting up to preach: "Open your imperfect Bible, please. I trust that our text is one of the texts that is perfect. Somewhere in this text we may cross an imperfect verse, but I don't know which one it is. But open your Bible that is full of errors, and let's see what God says."

When every one of those professors left home as preacher boys and went off to Bible college, they were carrying a King James Bible. Four years later when they graduated, they carried an *American Standard Version* home with them.

Let's review and make a logical choice. God promised to preserve His words for all generations. So somewhere there must be a perfect Bible that contains the pure words of God for our generation. The theologians say that only the original manuscripts contain the perfect words of God. Do we believe the theologians who say we have no perfect Bible, or do we believe God who promised to preserve His words to all generations? I choose to believe God.

Now I must choose which Bible is the Word of God. Do I choose the Bibles taken from the *Alexandrian* and *Catholic manuscripts* such as the ASV, the NASV, the RSV, and all the other so-called Bibles? Do I choose the Bibles that attack the deity of Christ, the plan of salvation through Christ, the virgin birth, and the blood of Christ? Do I choose the Bibles that have to be corrected regularly with new versions for the pocketbooks of publishers? Or do I choose the King James Bible— the One used in every great revival in history, the one used by every great soul-winning church, the one used by every great pastor in history, the one my mama used, the one used by D.L. Moody and Charles Spurgeon, and the one that has stood the test of time? The King James Bible is the only logical choice.

There is a perfect English Bible—the King James Bible.

Chapter Two

Final Authority

We must have a final authority. We must have some place in this world to find out God's principles. There must be a final authority. The final authority in the United States is the Supreme Court. Congress can pass all the laws they want, but the Supreme Court can nullify any of those laws. In the same way, God has to have a final authority whereby we can find the principles by which we are supposed to live.

Romans 12:1-2 says. *"I beseech you therefore, brethren, by the mercies of God, that ye present your bodies a living sacrifice, holy, acceptable unto God, which is your reasonable service. And be not conformed to this world: but be ye transformed by the renewing of your mind, that ye may prove what is that good, and acceptable, and perfect, will of God."*

For a person to find the perfect will of God, he must have a perfect command from God. If God has a perfect will for an individual's life, then God must reveal perfectly that will to him. It must be a perfect revelation of that will. If it is not a perfect revelation of the will of God, then a person cannot do the perfect will of God because he does not know what the perfect will of God is.

Sometimes, we Baptist people are almost charismatic. We talk too much about how "God led me to do thus and so." The truth is, practically everything that God ever leads anybody to do is written in the Bible. Please don't misunderstand me. God tells you in the Bible what kind of person you are supposed to marry. He will not choose anyone for you outside the circumferences He describes in the Bible. If you marry one of the "kind" God wants you to marry, then you are not far wrong. According to Philippians 2:5, God will control your mind to make the right decision. *"Let this mind be in you, which was also in Christ Jesus."* When it comes to the will of God for my life, I would ten thousand times rather check the Bible to find out the principle by which I am supposed to make a decision, and then ask God to control my mind while I make that decision. That's a lot better than saying, "Lord, lead me." He has already led you to the right pea patch, now you just have to figure out which row you have to pick. God would not be too upset if you pick peas on the wrong row as long as you are picking peas in the right pea patch.

So often our Hyles-Anderson College preacher boys come to me and say, "Brother Hyles, I need God to lead me where He wants me to go."

I tell them, "He's already told you to go into all the world. Pick a spot out in the world, and you can't be far from right."

I have an idea that if God wants a preacher to be in Kentucky and he ends up in Utah and wins Salt Lake City to Christ, God won't be too upset about that. If you Hyles-Anderson College students would spend as much time in the Bible as you spend begging God about where to go, He would come nearer telling you where to go. The first thing you have to do is learn the Bible so you know where the pea patch is. Then you go to the pea patch, find which row when you get there, and if you get in the wrong row, keep on picking. God won't keep you from it.

I'm simply saying, God is more concerned about a person obeying the **principle** than the **specific**. Inside the **principle**,

God will control a person's mind to make the **specific** decision. So you must find the principle. When you find the principle, many possibilities are automatically eliminated. The decision you have to make is confined to the circumference of the principle. Again, we have to find the principle. To find the principle, we must have a final authority.

There are only a few possibilities for our final authority:

1. The church—Catholicism. The Catholics say the church is the final authority. They could care less about what the Bible says. If the church says something, it's true to them. Any honest Catholic priest will tell you that the Catholic position on the final authority is that the Catholic church has the final authority. If you want to go further than that, Catholics believe that if the Pope speaks ex cathedra, he speaks as God, and the Pope is the final authority.

2. The mind—Humanism. The mind deciding what is right and wrong is humanism. That philosophy means that I am perfectly capable myself of deciding what is true and what is not true. Genesis 3:4-5 says, "*And the serpent said unto the woman, Ye shall not surely die*: [That is the first revised version of the Bible. God said that the moment you eat, you shall surely die, and Satan said, 'Ye shall not surely die.'] *For God doth know that in the day ye eat thereof, then your eyes shall be opened, and ye shall be as gods, knowing good and evil.*" In verse 5, the word "*knowing*" does not mean a person will find out what good and evil is; it means "he will know what it is; he himself determines what is good and what is evil." The Bible says, you yourself will be "*as gods, knowing good and evil.*"

That is exactly what modern theology is all about. The average college or seminary in America teaches that the individual can search for the truth. Liberals say that every man is searching for the truth, and every man gets a portion of the truth; nobody is wrong, and nobody is right.

We are all searching. Brother, you don't have to search for

the truth! We've found the truth!

Teenagers will say, "I don't see anything wrong with rock music." Well, teenager, according to Genesis 3:5, you think you are a god. No one has the right to determine what is good or evil, or he becomes the final authority. When any person says, "I don't see anything wrong with…," he is determining what good and evil is, and he is saying that God reveals His truth to a person through his mind. But no human can know good and evil because the human mind is not the final authority.

Isaiah 53:6 says, *"All we like sheep have gone astray; we have turned every one to his own way…."* What does that verse mean? It means that whatever my mind can comprehend is to me, the final authority.

Some self-styled intellectuals will say, "I just don't believe that a just God would send anybody to burn forever in Hell, so there is no Hell," or "It doesn't make sense to me that God would regenerate anybody, so there's no such thing as regeneration. What I can't conceive, I won't believe. What I can't understand, I won't accept." He is a humanist! He's playing God! He is his own idol.

Ninety-five percent of all religious colleges in America believe that the final authority is the human mind or human reasoning. To whatever degree the Bible is not believed, that society has the exact proportionate belief in humanism. If God hasn't told us what to do, man has to tell us what to do. When a country does not believe the Bible, it is totally humanistic.

3. The heart—Pentecostalism. Enter the charismatic who says, "I have a word of knowledge." Nothing in this world is as rotten to the core as the charismatic movement. One of those rascals on the television says, "I have a word of knowledge. I see a lady out there with a goiter on her neck," or "Someone out there has a pimple on his gall bladder," or "I had a vision." That practice is as rotten as liberalism! They are saying that their heart is their final authority. That is heresy. They are saying, "God is speaking to me." God has already spoken to them!

This could also include any Baptist who says, "I'm going to move to another area because the Lord is leading me." Of course, there's no red-hot church in that area, but he is getting a raise in pay. No one ever says, "God is leading me to take a cut in pay and move somewhere else." We've got charismatic thinking in our Baptist churches.

4. A man—Cultism. Cult believers will blindly follow a man. We have seen examples of cultists in Waco, Texas. Another example is the Catholic church; The Catholics blindly follow whatever "El Papa" says.

5. A group of men—Evangelicalism. A group of men get together and say, "We can improve what the Bible says."

The church, the mind, the heart, a man, or a group of men cannot be the final authority. Whatever our final authority is, it must be perfect. It cannot lead us to do the perfect will of God unless it is a perfect revelation of that will. Is the church perfect? No, the church is composed of men. Can an imperfect church lead anyone to the perfect will of God? No. Is the mind perfect? No. How about the heart, is the heart perfect? No. In Jeremiah 17:9, the Bible says, *"The heart is deceitful...and desperately wicked...."* Is there a perfect man? No. The Bible says in Romans 3:23, *"For all have sinned, and come short of the glory of God"* and in Romans 3:10, *"There is none righteous, no, not one."* Those verses include the Pope. There is no perfect man. Can a group of men be perfect? No. Ruling out the church, the mind, the heart, a man, or a group of men leaves us with only one other alternative: **a written revelation.**

6. A written revelation—the Bible. Man has to find a written revelation that is perfect. II Timothy 3:16 says, *"All scripture...."* What does *"all scripture"* mean? Since II Timothy 3:16 doesn't say **"every"** Scripture, the verse means that it must be a complete bundle. God is talking about the **complete** Scripture—every Scripture all together. II Timothy 3:16-17, "*All scripture is given by inspiration of God, and is profitable for doctrine* [teaching], *for reproof* [rebuking], *for correction* [restoring], *for instruction* [training] *in righteousness: That the man of God may be made perfect, throughly furnished unto all good works.*" These verses mean we need the complete Scripture. The word *profitable* is the key word in these verses. The word *unprofitable* means "garbage, refuse that is thrown away, discarded food, or human dung." If the word *unprofitable* means "garbage," then if **all** Scripture is profitable, there is one written revelation that contains no garbage. Therefore, since one written revelation is profitable, those which disagree with that profitable one, are unprofitable. Those that are unprofitable are garbage and as rotten as human dung.

Verse 16 says, "*All scripture is given by inspiration of God....*" If "*all scripture*" means "the total of Scripture," then would every book in that "*all scripture*" be inspired? Would every chapter in every book of that "*all scripture*" be inspired? Would every verse in every chapter in every book of that "*all scripture*" be inspired? Then would every word in every verse in every chapter in every book in that "*all scripture*" be inspired? Yes!

Have you ever picked up a set of instructions about 1:00 Christmas morning to assemble that electric train and instead find the instructions of how to assemble an electric razor? Nothing is more frustrating at 1:00 on Christmas morning than having the wrong instructions.

Knowing the perfect will of God means you've got to know exactly everything God wants you to do. You cannot know the perfect will of God unless He instructs you. He cannot instruct you through a church; the church is imperfect. He cannot instruct you through your mind; your mind is imperfect. He cannot instruct you through your heart; your heart is imperfect. He cannot instruct you through a man; all men are imperfect. He cannot instruct you through a group of men; they are imperfect. Neither can God instruct you through an imperfectly written revelation.

Suppose just one book in the Bible is wrong? Is that book garbage? Suppose one chapter is wrong; is that chapter garbage? Suppose one verse is wrong; is that verse garbage? Suppose one word is wrong; is that word garbage?

You say, "Brother Hyles, do you mean if there is just one word wrong in the Bible, you have to throw everything else away?" That's exactly what I mean!

You say, "Why don't we take all the rest of it and not take that one word?" You just went back to **your mind,** because now your mind has to decide what that one wrong word is.

The only authority that we as independent Baptists have is the Bible. There was a day when I could just say Baptist, but the truth is that most Southern Baptist colleges and seminaries are staffed by professors who don't believe that the Bible is the final authority. I could not recommend a single Southern Baptist college or seminary to anyone. None! Thirty-five years ago, when I attended a Southern Baptist college and seminary, I heard a professor say that he didn't believe in the Resurrection. He said that to him the Resurrection was a bunch of blindfolded spirits in a vacuum. If he made that statement 35 years ago, just think what they are saying now!

Consequently, we believe that the only final authority for practice and doctrine of the Christian and the church is the Bible. As an independent Baptist preacher, I cannot speak *ex cathedra.* I cannot say, "I'm going to speak now, and God is speaking through me." I can only speak and say that the Bible is true. I have no power but the power of influence. (Sometimes I wish I had power to make Christians live like I think they should live.)

It was a good day for me when I decided that I was going

to make the Word of God my final authority. I was "roboted" in Southern Baptist schools to believe that the Southern Baptist program was the final authority. One day, I decided to read my Bible and reorganize my church according to the Bible. I decided to read word for word the book of Acts and see what the New Testament church was all about. I cast aside all the traditions I had been taught, all the jargon I had been taught, and all of the catechism to which I had been taught to swear allegiance, and I decided that I was going to try to find out what kind of church the New Testament church really was.

I decided that what the New Testament church in Acts had scripturally was what I was going to have in my church. I believe that the First Baptist Church of Hammond is as near as is humanly possible to what the church in Jerusalem was 2,000 years ago. Why are we scattered abroad all over the Chicago area winning souls? Because the church in Jerusalem was scattered abroad everywhere. Why do we go from house to house knocking on doors? Because in Acts 5:42 the Bible says, "*And daily in the temple, and in every house, they ceased not to teach and preach Jesus Christ.*"

Dr. Curtis Hutson gave the best compliment to the First Baptist Church of Hammond when he said, "If God were writing the book of Acts today, He would write about the First Baptist Church of Hammond." I believe that is the ultimate compliment.

Some say that there are different types of churches such as the soul-winning churches and deeper-life churches. No, we have a church and they do not. The Bible is a church's charter to exist, and if the Bible is not the church's final authority in practice and doctrine, then you are not a church. You may have the word "church" on the sign outside, but you are not a church.

Follow my logic in these observations:

1. There must be a God. If any man will admit to me that he believes there is a God, I believe that if he will logically follow me, I can win him to Christ.

2. If there is a God, He must know who I am. If He is God, certainly He knows His creatures.

3. If there is a God and He knows me, then He must want to reveal Himself to me. Nobody would want to love someone and that someone not know who he was.

4. If God wants to reveal Himself to me, He must reveal Himself to me in a manner that I can understand.

5. Therefore, to reveal Himself to me in a manner that I would understand, He must reveal Himself to me as a man because that is all that I can understand.

6. If God wants to reveal Himself to me, then He must want me with Him.

7. If God wants me with Him, He must have made a way whereby I can be with Him.

8. Being His child, God must want what is best for me.

9. If He wants what is best for me, there must be a revelation from God of what is best for me. He has to get it to me.

10. However, He reveals to me what is best for me must be pure and perfect. If it is not pure and perfect, then I cannot know purely and perfectly what He wants for me.

God has a perfect (complete) will with intricate plans for your life. He must get those plans from His mind to your mind. How will He do it? "He does it through the church," says the Catholic. "He does it through the mind," says the humanist. "He does it through the heart," says the charismatic. "He does it through a man," says the cultist. "He does it through a group of men," says the new evangelical. They are all wrong! God revealed His perfect will through a perfect, written revelation, **the Bible—our final authority.**

Chapter Three

How We Got God's Words

I was once asked, "Okay, how did we get our Bible?" I thought, "Good night, I've been preaching on the Bible and hollering and screaming and waving the King James Bible for so long, but how did the words of God get to us?"

I don't mind it when we say, "I believe the Word of God." I think that statement is fine, but I like better the word "words" of God. There's nothing wrong with the statement, "The Bible is the Word of God. I like it better to say, "This Bible contains the words of God." There are at least four ideas about biblical inspiration.

First, some liberals believe the Bible was inspired, much like Shakespeare was inspired or John Milton was inspired or Fanny Crosby was inspired. That is the liberals' definition of "the inspiration of the Scriptures." Those rascals will also use our fundamentalist terminology to try to give their position so they can work their way inside our institutions.

Secondly, some believe that God gave men the thoughts that He had, and men put down the thoughts in their own words. Of course, that is a very dangerous doctrine. In other words, Paul wrote in a certain style; Peter wrote in a certain style; and Isaiah wrote in a certain style; so these men must have written in their own words the thoughts that God gave to them. I'd like to announce that before Paul was made, the Word was made. God didn't give Paul a certain kind of words to fit him. God made a man like Paul to fit the words that were eternal, already in Heaven. So, the idea of inspiration that God gave man the thoughts and man wrote down the words in his own language is deadly, dangerous, and godless.

Thirdly, some believe that God gave men the words, and men gave the words to us. I do not believe this idea of biblical inspiration either. I do not believe that God gave to men the words, and then men in turn gave them to us. I would not mind someone else believing that idea. I simply do not believe that idea myself.

Lastly, some believe in verbal inspiration. Let me explain this idea.

1. The words of God always have been. Psalm 119:89 says, *"For ever, O LORD, thy word is settled in heaven."* This verse means there always was the entire Bible in Heaven. The word *settled* means "finished." The Bible was "finished" forever; it always has been. Now we can't understand that truth, but there always has been God. There always has been the Son of God. There always has been the Word of God. Before John was born, the book of John was written in Heaven. Before Isaiah was born, the book of Isaiah was written in Heaven. Before the books of I and II Peter were written by Peter, these books were written already in Heaven. The words of God have always been.

2. Man must have those words. In Matthew 4:4 when Jesus said, *"…It is written…,"* the Devil was tempting Him on the mount of temptation. Jesus did not use His own wiles and ways to resist the temptation of the Devil. He used the Word of God. Three times the Devil tempted Jesus, and three times Jesus said, *"It is written…."* *"But he answered and said, It is written, Man shall not live by bread alone, but by every word that proceedeth out of the mouth of God."* Man must have the words of

God, and every word is important; therefore, there must be a place and a way that man can get "…*every word that proceedeth out of the mouth of God,*" or every one of the words of the Word of God. That is why every word is important.

Verbal inspiration means that the Bible contains the **words** of God, not the **thoughts** of God. Man cannot live except "…*by every word that proceedeth out of the mouth of God.*" I'm sorry, but the *Reader's Digest Version* is just not enough. The verse, "…*every word that proceedeth out of the mouth of God,*" does not say that man must live by every **thought** that proceedeth out of the mind of the Father.

The head of the Department of Bible at an nondenominational university said, "We have no perfect English Bible." What is the difference in a fellow making that statement at a non-denominational Bible college or at Harvard University? "…*Man shall not live by bread alone, but by every word*…." I am not fighting these universities; I am fighting these liberal professors. We must have **every** word, so there has to be a perfect English Bible or we cannot live.

3. God must find a way to get those words that have always been in Heaven to us. A Christian can only live "…*by every word that proceedeth out of the mouth of God.*"

4. God chose men and made them holy. Luke 1:70 says, "*As he spake by the mouth of his holy prophets, which have been since the world began.*" II Peter 1:20-21 says, "*Knowing this first, that no prophecy of the scripture is of any private interpretation. For the prophecy came not in old time by the will of man: but holy men of God spake as they were moved by the Holy Ghost.*"

Notice the words "*holy prophets*" in Luke and "*holy men of God*" in II Peter. These men were not holy before they were chosen to be used to get the words of God to us. The word *holy* in the Bible does not mean "holy, in the sense of perfect men, good men." It means "holy, in the sense of men who were chosen for a particular job." In the Bible, the word *holy* means "sanctified," and the word *sanctified* means "set apart for a unique purpose." For example, my pulpit is holy. It is set apart for the preaching and the teaching of the Word of God. It is not a perfect pulpit, but it is a holy pulpit.

God is not saying that He chose the best men. I don't think in some cases that God chose the best men to give us the Bible. These were not perfect men or maybe, even in some cases, they were not even above average men. God did not choose holy men to give us His words. He chose men and made them holy, meaning He set them apart.

God chose David. Was David a holy man? No! David was an adulterer and a murderer, but He was one of the men who penned a good deal of the Bible. Was Moses a holy man? No! Moses was also a murderer. God is not saying He chose men who were above other men or better than other men; He chose certain men by His own wisdom and His own desire and set those men apart to deliver to us the words that are in Heaven.

Perfection can flow through imperfection. There are two "words of God." The Bible is the **written** Word of God, and Jesus is the **living** Word of God. John 1:1 says, *"In the beginning was the Word, and the Word was with God, and the Word was God."* Jesus was called, *the Word of God* and the Bible is the Word of God. My Saviour came from the womb of an imperfect person. Jesus, the living Word, was conceived in and flowed through an imperfect vessel. If the **living** Word can flow through imperfection, why can't the **written** Word?

So, in Heaven are the words of God; on earth is man. Matthew 4:4 says, *"...Man shall not live by bread alone, but by every word that proceedeth out of the mouth of God."* God had to get those words to us, so God chose men and made them holy. When God made them holy, it doesn't mean He made them better than anybody else or that they already were better than anybody else. It simply means that these men were set apart for the task of giving to us the words that were already in Heaven.

5. God gave the words in Heaven to man through these chosen men of God. God could not give to sinful man the words to give to us. Do you think God is going to give murderer David His words and say, "David, you give the very words I give you." No. God did not give those words in Heaven to men to give to us. God Himself gave us those words in Heaven **through** these men. God didn't say, "David, here are My words. You give them to the world." No, God said, "David, open your mouth. I'm going to **breathe** words through you." God gave the words not **to** these men but **through** these men.

When I talk to you, I am breathing. It is my breathing that gives me the breath that goes across my vocal cords, and coming toward you is my talking to you. When God breathed the words through these men, He didn't say, "Here are the words. Write them down." No, God said, "Open your mouth, and the words are going to come through you, but I'm going to speak them through your mouth." God breathed words through chosen holy men of old so that they could give us the words in Heaven that we may be able to live.

Acts 1:16 says, *"Men and brethren, this scripture must needs have been fulfilled, which the Holy Ghost by the mouth of David spake...."* This verse didn't say, "by the brain of David" or "by the mind of David." These words in Heaven didn't get to us through the mind of David, down to the mouth of David, and out to us. God sent those words, bypassed David's brain, and breathed them through David's mouth. God used David's mouth to give us eternal words. Why? God surely would not want to trust a cursing Apostle Peter who denied the Lord, who denied the faith, who denied the church, and then say, "Peter, here are My words; go give them to the people." No, sir! He said, "Peter, you open your mouth, and I will use your mouth as a tool through which My words can come from Me." The Bible is not men giving us the words of God. It is God Himself giving us the words using the mouth of the men who were chosen by God to do so.

II Samuel 23:2 states, *"...his word was in my tongue."* The self-acclaimed intelligentsia and the self-acclaimed theologians are proud of the fact that they can teach the Bible to God every day. These men like to call those of us who believe in a God-breathed Bible ignoramuses. They teach that God gave the words to chosen men, and these men gave it to us.

Solomon wrote part of the Bible. Would you trust a man who married 700 wives and had 300 substitutes in case one of the others got sick? Do you want to trust that person to give you God's words? Not me! God said, "Solomon, I'm **not** going to use your brain; I'm going to use your mouth."

David says in Psalm 45:1, *"My heart is inditing a good matter: I speak of the things which I have made touching the king: my tongue is the pen of a ready writer."* David was saying, "My tongue is God's pen." I hold in my hand a pen. I do not know where this pen came from. It may have been given to me by a bootlegger, but I can still use it to write my words. David was saying, "I am just the pen." David was not the penman; he was the pen. God did not give His words to Solomon, a wicked polygamist, an adulterer, and a whoremonger. God did not say to him, "Solomon, I want to give you some words to give the people." No, sir! He said, "Solomon, You're My pen. I am the Penman."

Notice these facts about the pen:

• **The pen may have previously written on other subjects.** No man in this world is righteous enough to be able to take the words of God Almighty, be the custodian of those words, and get those words to us. Much of the Bible was written by three murderers: David, Moses, and Paul. I'm not willing to say, and certainly God was not willing to say, "I am going to trust these mortal creatures to deliver My words." Not one living piece of flesh in this world is capable of adequately being the custodian of those words in Heaven, as well as getting those words to men down on the earth.

• **The pen does not decide what it writes.** The human brain decides what the pen writes; however, regarding the Bible, man did not decide what he wrote. The writers were pens, and God was the Penman. These holy men, which means they were separated, chosen for the task, were not better men.

I carry two pens. I decide the use of these pens. When I write to you, these pens are not saying a thing to you. David said, "I am God's pen." The pen may have been used to write on other subjects or the pen may have a bad past. The pen is not the issue; all that matters is the author.

3. God used all kinds of pens. He chose a fisherman who, during the darkest hours of the life of Christ—the death of Christ—denied that he belonged to the church, denied that he belonged to the faith, denied that he belonged to Jesus, and cursed and swore. He was one of those holy men of old. God used all kinds of men as pens. It's not the just men who gave us the Bible because they were not always just. It is the just God who gave us the Bible and used unjust men as pens to write down the Bible. Some modern theologians call that "mechanical dictation," and use that explanation to try to prove that fundamentalists are unintelligent.

Let me share an example. My first part-time secretary had previously worked as Dr. W. A. Criswell's secretary at First Baptist Church in Dallas. She moved to Garland and joined our church. I hired her ever so briefly. One day, I personally dictated some letters to her. She typed the letters and returned them to me for my signature. Those letters looked strange to me; they didn't sound like me. I took them back to her and asked, "Are these my words?"

She said, "This is what you gave me."

I said, "Get out your dictation pad and read me what's on the dictation pad."

She said, "I was Dr. Criswell's secretary, and you're a young preacher. Dr. Criswell's a wise man. I used some of his terminology instead of yours."

I said, "You can go back to work for him. You're fired." She left immediately and never came back.

God Almighty was the One Who gave us these words, and He was not willing to trust human flesh such as John. Though John forsook Jesus and fled when Jesus was being tried, John wrote I John, II John, III John, Revelation, and the Gospel of John. John and James had their mother come and talk to Jesus to see if they could get special favors from Him.

I believe with all of my heart that these were great men, but I do not believe that they were great enough to be the deliverers of the very words in Heaven to man. We must have them. You can't make a mistake, Peter! You can't make a mistake, John! You can't make a mistake, Jeremiah! You can't make a mistake, Isaiah! Why? Because every word that is in Heaven has to get to me. If I live, I have to have every word that is there. I'm sorry; I'm not going to trust you, Peter—you cursing, denying apostle. I'm not going to trust you to get those words in Heaven to me. God said, "Neither am I. I'll just use his mouth. I'll use Peter as a pen, and I'll write the words Myself."

The words of God were given to us by God and not by holy men. They were given to us by God **through** holy men, using them to get the words to us. Sometimes that pen didn't understand all he wrote. References in the Bible reveal how that some of these men did not know exactly what they were writing. Why? They were just pens; the Penman was doing the writing! God's voice gave His Word **through** them, not **to** them.

"Brother Hyles, so what if a preacher boy goes down to a so-called Christian college where he sits in a liberal professor's class who teaches, 'We have no perfect Bible.' What difference does it make?" It makes all the difference in the world! What that preacher better do is take the Bible rather than some institution to which he subscribes his loyalty. What he better do is stop and realize that if we have no perfect English Bible, we cannot live because "...*Man shall not live by bread alone, but by every word that proceedeth out of the mouth of God.*" (Matthew 4:4)

If I did not believe that every word in the Bible had been preserved from the time it was given through the mouth of men as God, the Penman, wrote with the pen of humanity, I would walk out of this pulpit, and I wouldn't waste my life preaching. If there's a word in the Bible that is wrong, no one knows which one it is, so it could be any of them. I believe that we have God's preserved words for us in the King James Bible. In conclusion, how did we get God's words?

1. The words of God were always in Heaven.
2. Man must have every word to live.
3. God had to find a way to get every word to man.
4. God chose men and made them *holy*, which means they were "set apart or chosen" to be God's pens.
5. God gave His words to us through those chosen men. God said, "I want you men to be My pens, and I will pick you up, and I will use you to write My words as the Penman. I will not use your brain; I will use your mouth." God gave us the God-breathed Book. God's breath across the vocal cords of human beings gave us His words.
6. God has preserved His words for us in the King James Bible.

Chapter Four

From Revelation to Illumination

What is meant when we say that we have the words of God? Psalm 12:6 says, *"The words of the LORD are pure words...."* These words were spoken by the Psalmist David hundreds of years after the first giving of Scripture to man. There were no originals at that time, so obviously the words had been preserved. *"The words of the LORD are pure words: as silver tried in a furnace of earth, purified seven times."* Verse six is saying that up to David's time, God had kept the words of the Lord pure. In verse seven, *"Thou shalt keep them, O LORD, thou shalt preserve them from this generation for ever,"* David is saying that God always will keep His words pure.

Psalm 68:11 says, *"The LORD gave the word: great was the company of those that published it."* This verse doesn't necessarily mean "many," but it does mean these were great men to whom God gave the Word. Psalm 119:89 states, *"For ever, O LORD, thy word is settled in heaven."*

Every generation has to redefine the Bible for itself. Every generation has to discover for itself that the King James Bible contains the words of God. Every generation has to experience a split because every movement experiences a natural deterioration. Everything has to die except the local church to which God has promised divine perpetuity. The local church may die, but it doesn't have to die. The biggest split that has ever come will come in the next ten years, if not sooner, over the King James Bible, and it couldn't come soon enough for me.

I'm tired of colleges and universities advertising that they use the King James Bible. Tell the whole story! Tell everyone that you do not believe that it is inspired word for word and that you use other fake Bibles also. Tell the whole story that you have some Bible professors and so-called theologians in your Bible department who believe that there are other so-called Bibles that are better than the King James Bible. Tell the whole story! The issue that is dividing Baptists in my generation is the healthiest issue ever, the Bible. What better issue could divide? We're not going to divide over some piddling issue. We are going to divide over the foundation of our faith; and that is, "What is the Word of God, and where is the Word of God?"

Let me explain what I mean when I say that the King James Bible contains the words of God. I believe that every word in the King James Bible is God's Word. The following five words explain the entire picture of the King James Bible being the words of God.

Revelation

There are four parts to revelation:

1. The Bible always was. Psalm 119:89 states, *"For ever, O LORD, thy word is settled in heaven."* That verse means that there never was a time that the Bible was not. The Bible is as old as God. The Bible is as pre-existent as Jesus Christ. The Bible always existed. That truth is hard for anyone to comprehend something that doesn't begin or doesn't end, but the truth is, the Bible never began, and it will never end. It is the eternal Word of God. The Bible always was.

2. God revealed the words of God to man as the words were in Heaven. God did not let men write the Book in their own personality; God created personalities in men to fit the book that was already written. The words of God were in Heaven before there was ever a world, before there was ever a river, before there was ever a sea, before there was ever a bird or fish or beast or flower or man. The words of the Lord have always existed. God revealed the Bible to holy men of old just as it was in Heaven.

Our scholarly friends who call themselves theologians (a theologian is a guy who gets together with a bunch of other guys and agrees to call themselves theologians) say, "If God gave it to man, word for word, that is mechanical dictation." If that is what you want to call God's method of revelation, call it that! I'm just telling you what it was. God said to Paul, "Paul, write down this word," and Paul wrote it down. God said, "Now write down the next word," and Paul wrote it down. God told Moses exactly word for word what to write. Every single word in the Bible has always existed; God simply gave it word for word to holy men of old. Just like the tabernacle in the wilderness was an exact replica of the tabernacle in Heaven, even so, the printed words in the Bible are exactly like those in Heaven today.

3. **While God was in the process of giving us the Bible that was already in Heaven, God found it necessary to give special instructions at times.** For example, consider the story of Balaam, a popular preacher. When he was invited by a wicked king to preach in that king's country, Balaam asked God if he should go. I would not have had to do that because I have II Corinthians 6:14 and following. Balaam couldn't turn his Bible to II Corinthians because Balaam did not have all of the revelation of God. He did not have all of the words of God available, so God gave Balaam some special instructions by divine revelation.

Another example was when God spoke audibly to Adam and Eve in the Garden of Eden. Why? Adam and Eve had no

Bible at all. They couldn't open their Bible to see what to do, so God spoke and told them what to do.

4. The more the written Word was revealed to man, the less God spoke audibly to man. In the Garden of Eden, the only way God spoke was audibly. Now, that we have the revealed Word of God, there's no need for God to speak audibly. I'd rather have the Bible with the words written down than for God to speak to me audibly because I might hear some voice that is not God's voice. I **know** the Bible contains God's words.

Adam couldn't turn to Matthew, Mark, Luke, or John. Adam couldn't turn to the prophets or the Psalm or the Proverbs. He didn't have them, but we have them all. We have God's total revelation in the Bible—every doctrine and every truth. We don't have to run to God and ask Him if we should go to some liberal university; it is written in the Book not to go. We don't have to ask God if we should date someone who is not a Christian; it is written in the Book not to do it. We don't have to ask somebody if we should drink liquor; God has already told us what to do. Don't be too upset with Noah for getting drunk; he didn't have the Psalm or Ephesians 5.

God has given us a set of instructions, the Word of God. Far too many of us are trying to get some special revelation from God when we have God's total written revelation right in our hands. All of the instructions we need for the Christian life are in the Bible.

Inspiration

II Timothy 3:16,17, "*All scripture is given by inspiration of God, and is profitable for doctrine, for reproof, for correction, for instruction in righteousness: That the man of God may be perfect, throughly furnished unto all good works.*" The word, *inspiration* means "God-breathed." Just as God breathed into man the breath of life, the Bible is God-breathed. In the original manuscripts, God inspired word for word what every man should write down. In the 1950's at Southwestern Seminary, I heard a professor say, "God did not give us the very words. God gave man the thoughts, and man penned those thoughts in his own words."

Little ol' Jackie-boy Hyles stood up and said, "That's a lie!" Every word was given by inspiration of God. II Peter 1:21 says, *"For the prophecy came not in old time by the will of man: but holy men of God spake as they were moved by the Holy Ghost."* Two words are used to explain *inspiration.* One is *verbal* which means "every word is inspired"; the other is *plenary* which means "all Scripture is inspired." In this study thus far, we've discussed only the original language. That leads me to the next word.

Preservation

God gave the Bible word for word and preserved it word for word. That is what Psalm 12:6 and 7 mean. *"The words of the LORD are pure words: as silver tried in a furnace of earth, purified seven times. Thou shalt keep them, O LORD, thou shalt preserve them from this generation for ever."* By breathing through holy men of old, God inspired the very words of God that were in Heaven. God said, "I want you to write what I tell you to write." God looked at the Book in Heaven and read it word for word to those men, and they wrote it word for word. The God who could do that could also preserve the very words that He inspired.

That means that the Bible I hold in my hands contains the very words of God Almighty. If I believed what most nondenominational so-called Bible colleges believe, I would close my Bible and never preach another sermon. If we do not have the words of God, we cannot preach the words of God. Don't tell me God would call me to preach His Word and not give me His words. Don't tell me that God would say, *"...Man shall* not live by bread alone, but by every word that proceedeth out of the mouth of God" and not give me every word. The Bible contains the very preserved words of God Almighty.

The Bible is just as infallible now as the moment God gave it. Jesus said 2,000 years ago in Matthew 5:18 that "one jot or one tittle shall in no wise pass from the law, till all be fulfilled." Jesus had no originals with Him. He was saying that every bit of the Bible that He had up until then had been preserved for 4,000 years. If God could preserve His Word for 4,000 years, He could make it for 2,000 more. We know it was preserved when Jesus was here because Jesus said it was.

I ask you theologians, "Did Jesus have the very words of God or not?" If I don't, He didn't! If God could preserve His words for 4,000 years when they had no printing presses at all, don't you think He could preserve the words of God for 2,000 years with our modern ways of printing?

I mentioned previously that God said to the church at Ephesus, "Put on the whole armour of God." The church at Ephesus was told to use only one offensive weapon. They had many defensive weapons, helmet, breastplate, girdle, shoes, and shield, but only one offensive weapon, the words of Almighty God. That's all.

Do you think the members in the church at Ephesus had more battles to fight than we do? Do you think God would give the church at Ephesus the very words of God and give His church today a counterfeit? Would God give them an M-1 rifle and give us a BB gun? We fight the same Devil they fought. We must have the same weapon they had.

We fight the same enemies, the same principalities, and the same powers they fought; therefore, we have to have the same weapon they had. If the people in the church at Ephesus had a perfect Bible with which to fight the Devil, I have to have a perfect Bible with which to fight the Devil.

Illumination

I Corinthians 2:9 says, "*But as it is written, Eye hath not seen, nor ear heard, neither have entered into the heart of man, the things which God hath prepared for them that love him.*" Primarily, this Scripture is not referring to Heaven but about the words of God. What does this verse mean? Man cannot understand the Bible by himself. Human eyes cannot understand the Bible. Human ears cannot understand the Bible. Neither human minds nor human hearts can understand the Bible because it is a spiritual book. Verses 10-14 say, "*But God hath revealed them unto us by his Spirit; for the Spirit searcheth all things, yea, the deep things of God. For what man knoweth the things of man, save the spirit of a man which is in him? even so the things of God knoweth no man, but the Spirit of God. Now we have received, not the spirit of the world, but the spirit which is of God; that we might know the things that are freely given to us of God. Which things also we speak, not in the words which man's wisdom teacheth, but which the Holy Ghost teacheth; comparing spiritual things with spiritual. But the natural man receiveth not the things of the Spirit of God: for they are foolishness unto him: neither can he know them....*"

It is tomfoolery for the natural men of the *Reader's Digest* to publish a Bible; they cannot understand the things of God. It is tomfoolery for the National Council of Churches, a bunch of degenerates who are probably not converted, to put out a Bible. They cannot understand the Word of God. Human eyes, ears, minds, and hearts cannot understand the Bible, but the Spirit of God understands the Word of God.

Verse 14 says, "*But the natural man receiveth not the things of the Spirit of God: for they are foolishness unto him: neither can he know them, because they are spiritually discerned.*" I call that discernment, illumination—meaning that the Holy Spirit Who revealed the Bible, inspired the Bible, and preserved the Bible also illuminates the Bible while we read it. It is the Holy Spirit Who teaches the Bible to us.

Let me illustrate. I was on an airplane for a one-hour flight. The plane was about 15 minutes into its flight when I looked across the aisle and noticed a lady sitting in the window seat reading. To my total shock, she was reading my book, *Blue Denim and Lace*. I'd never before seen anyone read one of my books in public. I asked, "Ma'am, is that a good book?"

She said, "I don't know. I can't understand it. Many chapters in this book are too deep for me, and I can't understand them. It's written by a guy named Hyles. I wish sometimes I could meet this guy and ask him some questions about what is in this book."

I said, "My name is Jack Hyles."

She said, "Would you come over and explain your book to me?" I moved over to the adjacent seat, and for almost an hour, I explained chapter after chapter. I was illuminating the chapters and lines that I had written.

In the same way, God has revealed to us His Word, inspired that Word, and preserved that Word, but that is not all. He has given us that same Holy Spirit Who wrote the Word to teach it to us. If you're not converted, you don't have that Holy Spirit, and you can't know the Bible. I don't care how easy translators make the words, a person is not going to understand the Bible unless the Spirit of God teaches it to him. We can understand the Bible, but only as the Holy Spirit teaches to us the Book that He wrote.

I, for one, believe that the Holy Spirit can do a better job of teaching the Bible than the theologians. Instead of making the Bible easier to read, why don't you find someone Who can teach what the difficult passages mean? The Holy Spirit can make it plainer than any theologian can, but perhaps the theologian doesn't have the Holy Spirit's help. The theologian is changing God's Book. He is meddling with God's Words. So to whom is the theologian making the Bible plainer?

My mother had a third-grade education, but the Holy Spirit taught her the Bible. She didn't need the theologians' help; she had the Author of the Bible living inside of her. The old country preachers who never saw the inside of a seminary and didn't know what a theologian was, lived in the Book and walked with God, and the Holy Spirit taught them the Bible. They didn't need a new version. The Author lived in them and taught His words to them.

Then who needs the words made easier? The scholars do. We "dumb bunnies" do not need any help because we have the Author. So leave the theologians alone; let them write themselves a Bible. They have no other help. I would not give you any hope for a man to be born of the Spirit of God who will change the Bible. Our country was a pretty good country before we started meddling with the Word of God. In this 20th century alone, over 100 new so-called Bibles have been published. Now comic book Bibles are being produced. Of course, the artists will make Abraham, all the Old Testament saints, and the Apostles look like hippies.

Whose job is it to make the Bible understood to us? The Holy Spirit. Do you think He needs any help? Then these men who are "making the Bible easier for us to understand" are playing Holy Spirit and doing His work. They are false teachers. Some have a hard time swallowing this truth because they have given their allegiance to some institution rather than principles.

Over 48 years ago, I told God I would live the rest of my life by five principles:

1. Money will never be an issue in my preaching.
2. Nobody will ever meddle with my preaching.
3. I'll make my decisions on the basis of right and wrong and not expediency.
4. I'll be a friend to my friends.

5. I will not give my loyalty to institutions.

I will give my loyalty to principles and support the institutions that embrace those principles. I've been saying that for over 48 years. Don't be surprised because I've dropped my loyalty to some institutions. The old preachers like Bob Jones, Sr.; John R. Rice; G. B. Vick; J. Frank Norris; and Bob Ketchum are gone. A new generation of young whippersnappers who didn't fight the war have come on the scene. They are peacetime soldiers who are trying to change the Word of God. To me that is like teenagers rebelling against their parents to have their own thinking and not embracing what is handed down to them by somebody else.

Interpretation

The Bible is an ever-fresh book. I study the Bible carefully for over 20 hours weekly; and yet, many times as I read the Scripture, the Holy Spirit will show me a truth I've never before noticed. John 16:13 says, *"Howbeit when he, the Spirit of truth, is come, he will guide you into all truth...."* The Bible says, *"all truth."* I guess you don't need another Bible after all!

There are two ridiculous extremes: On one end are those who say that they are going back to the original language to change the Bible so you can have the truth. On the other end, are the charismatics who are getting "it" from God afresh and anew when you others do not get "it" from God that way. Why doesn't somebody just get the Bible and say, "Holy Spirit, teach the Bible to me while I read it." That's what Mama did.

John 16:13 continues, *"...all truth, for he shall not speak of himself."* Show me a group of people who talk more about the Holy Spirit than they do about Jesus, and I'll show you a group of people who don't know much about the Holy Spirit. My Bible says that He won't speak of Himself. The Holy Spirit speaks of Jesus. *"... but whatsoever he shall hear, that shall he speak: and he will shew you things to come."*

II Peter 1:20 says, "*Knowing this first, that no prophecy of the scripture is of any private interpretation.*" That verse means that anyone can know the Bible as well as another. The Holy Spirit can teach a saved junior-age boy better than He can teach an unsaved theologian.

Conclusion

Let's review: The Holy Spirit revealed God's Word to us. While He was revealing His words, He spoke audibly on occasion. He spoke less audibly as more of the written words were given to us until He gave us the entire written Word; that is **revelation**. The Holy Spirit was the One Who inspired it and breathed it into holy men of old; that is **inspiration**.

That revelation which God inspired has been preserved as He said He would preserve it for these 6,000 years, which means we still have those very words; that is **preservation**. In order for us to learn what the words of God mean, we do not need someone to make the words easier. We need the Holy Spirit to teach us, He comes along and enters into our bodies at salvation, and teaches what God had in mind while we read it; that's **illumination**. Then He leads us to other Scriptures and compares Scriptures and helps us to find the truth—**interpretation**.

If you want systematic theology, get Grandma to read the Bible, and ask the Lord to teach it to her while she reads it. My Uncle Roy was a farmer who sharecropped 40 acres. In the winter time, he would sit beside the wood stove and read his Bible by the hour. My Uncle Roy knew the Bible. I promise you that you could talk about any part of the Bible and my Uncle Roy could teach it to you. He'd never met a theologian. He'd never seen a *Revised Standard Version*. The NASV and the NIV had not yet been published; and still, my Uncle Roy knew the Bible. Why? Because the One Who revealed, inspired, preserved, illuminates, and interprets the Bible lived inside my Uncle Roy.

So, saint of God who doesn't know any Greek, just open the old King James Bible and look up to God and say, "I'm going to read it; now You teach it to me." That is the best form of Bible study any person will ever have. You don't have to have Scofield's notes; after all, Apostle Paul didn't look at Scofield's notes very often. Paul didn't even have a Scofield Reference Bible. You don't even need a Bible dictionary or a thesaurus. All you really need is to fall in love with the Bible and read it and read it and read it. As you do, ask the Holy Spirit Who dwells inside you to illumine the Bible to you. The Bible will come alive as He illumines and interprets His words.

Chapter Five

God Is No Respecter of Persons

Acts 10:33, 34, "*Immediately therefore I sent to thee; and thou hast well done that thou art come. Now therefore are we all here present before God, to hear all things that are commanded thee of God. Then Peter opened his mouth, and said, Of a truth I perceive that God is no respecter of persons.*" This verse means that man determines his own destiny. This verse also means that God does not show partiality to a certain generation or to a certain part of the world. God sees all men together. Romans 3:23 says, "*For all have sinned, and come short of the glory of God.*" Christ died for everybody.

Ephesians 6:12-17 states, "*For we wrestle not against flesh and blood, but against principalities, against powers, against the rulers of the darkness of this world, against spiritual wickedness in high places. Wherefore take unto you the whole armour of God, that ye may be able to withstand in the evil day, and having done all, to stand. Stand therefore, having your loins girt about with truth, and having on the breastplate of righteousness; And your feet shod with the preparation of the gospel of peace; Above all, taking the shield of faith, wherewith ye shall be able to quench all the fiery darts of the wicked. And take the helmet of salvation, and the sword of the Spirit, which is the word of God.*"

In this battle against the Devil, the Christian has only one offensive weapon, the Bible. God gave him only one weapon. If you preachers think you are going to go out and build a church on your personality, you've got another think coming. Two thousand years after this passage was written, Christians still have the same enemy, the Devil. Christians today have the same opposition, the principalities and powers. We fight the same battle, and the only weapon is the Word of God.

Now, let me reason with you. Do you think that if God is not a respecter of persons that He would give to the first generation a sword and give to this generation a penknife? We fight the same battle, and we have the same enemy. The Bible says we have the same weapon, the Sword of the Spirit. If God did not preserve His Word and if the only words of God are in the original manuscripts, then this generation does not have as sharp a Sword as the first generation had. The first generation had the perfect words of God, but we do not. If that be true, then we are trying to fight the enemy with a penknife like the first generation fought with the Sword. We're going out to fight with a Sword that has pits on it. We're going out to fight with a Sword that was only good in the original. If this premise is correct and if God did not preserve His Word, then God gave the people who lived during the time of the original manuscripts a perfect Sword, and He gave 20th-century Christians an imperfect Sword. That situation doesn't sound like God is no respecter of persons. The truth is, God is no respecter of persons, so God would not send us out to fight the same enemy without the same Sword. God would not give us a dull, tainted Sword to fight the same enemy in the same battles, as an earlier generation.

In Ephesians 5:25, 26, the Word of God is called *water.* *"...Christ also loved the church, and gave himself for it; That He might sanctify and cleanse it with the washing of water by the word."* This verse means that whatever the Word of God was then, God called it water. God said that the church is washed by water—the Word of God. That means Christians to wash themselves with the Bible. It is the cleanser. The Psalmist said, "*Wherewithal shall a young man cleanse his way?....*" If God is no respecter of persons and we have to be cleansed by the washing of the water of the Word of God, then God would have to give us water that is just as clean as He gave to the Psalmist. God would not give one generation pure water and another a muddy pond.

Show me a church that does not believe the King James Bible, and I'll show you a church that is not as clean as a church that believes the King James Bible. Show me a church with a pastor who preaches the NIV, and I'll show you a church that is not as separated as the First Baptist Church of Hammond.

If God did not preserve the Words of the Bible, then He is a respecter of persons, but the Bible says that God is no respecter of persons. The same sins that Christians faced 2,000 years ago are the same sins we face today. They had the same temptations as we do; therefore, we need the same Cleanser that they had. God is duty-bound to give a Bible that is just as clean and pure as the Christians had in the days that the Word of God was given.

In Jeremiah 23:29, the Word of God is called a hammer. "*Is not my word...like a hammer that breaketh the rock into pieces?*" That verse means that the Bible is a builder. How do you build a church? You build it on the Bible. The first Wednesday night that I was pastor of the First Baptist Church of Hammond, 40 people attended the service. I started with Genesis 1:1 and began teaching the Word of God. I've had no Fall Programs, contests, or prizes to promote for Wednesday night crowds. I just announced that every Wednesday night I was going to teach the Bible. This Bible has built the largest Wednesday night crowd in the world. The Bible is the builder, and the churches that believe the King James Bible are the great, growing, soul-winning churches in the world today. Some of my Baptist friends, many about my age, now use the NIV. When they only believed and used the King James Bible, their churches were growing, and people were saved by the hundreds.

If you want to be clean, then get the Bible. If you want to build a church or a home or anything that is right and decent that will last, the Bible is the builder. It's the hammer. Would God give one generation a sledge hammer and another generation a tack hammer? Can a just God not be a respecter of persons?

Every preacher whom I know who does not believe there is a perfect Bible, and who claims to preach the Gospel went off to college with a King James Bible. Some dirty professor tampered with him and shook his faith in the Book from which his pastor preached, from which his mama read to him, and the one that he had when he went to college. That preacher went to college with the King James Bible but came back with the NIV or ASV.

God would not give one generation a sledge hammer to build with but the next generation a tack hammer; otherwise, He is not a just God. God is duty bound to give me the same weapon He gave the New Testament Church. God is duty bound to give me the same cleanser He gave the New Testament Church. God is duty bound to give me the same builder He gave the New Testament Church.

The Word of God is called a fire in Jeremiah 23:29. "*Is not my word like as a fire?...*" Would God give one generation a pillar of fire and another generation a spark? If the King James Bible is not as true as the one the Apostle Paul held in his hands; then he had a fire, and I've got a spark. The preachers in this world who are on fire for God have in their hands a King James Bible. Visit the churches that don't believe that the King James Bible is the preserved Word of God and see how much fire they have. Young preachers, don't believe and follow some professor who doesn't have any fire at all. If you do, you'll lose your fire. You'll lose your zeal. You'll lose your fervor. Stick with the Book that's a fire!

The Word of God is called a lamp and a light in Psalm 119:105. *"Thy word is a lamp unto my feet, and a light unto my path."* Would God give one generation a floodlight but give another generation a candle? Is that the kind of God you have? Do you have the kind of God Who would give to a generation 2,000 years ago a better Bible than you have? Is your God so weak that He could not preserve His words? Could not the God Who gave His words to holy men of old preserve His words for our generation?

Would God give one generation a sword but another generation a penknife? Would God give one generation pure water but another generation a mud hole? Would God give one generation a sledgehammer but another generation a tack hammer? Would God give one generation a pillar of fire but another generation a small spark?

If you want to build a great church, then you build it on the King James Bible. Show me the bus ministries of the churches that don't use the King James Bible. You say, "I know one." While you know of one, I know a thousand that have great bus ministries that use the King James Bible. Show me the churches with street ministries, homeless ministries, rescue mission ministries, and the poor ghetto ministries; I'll show you a church using the King James Bible. The churches that are on fire for God are King James Bible churches.

The Bible says that the Word of God shows us His will. It's a lamp unto my feet to show me His will today and a light unto my path to show me His will tomorrow. Would God be more desirous to show the first-century Christians His will than He would be to show the twentieth-century Christians His will? If so, then God is a respecter of persons. God is showing favoritism. Do you mean to tell me that today's Christians have a diluted, second-class, second-rate, imperfect lamp to show us the will of God? I don't serve a God like that! I serve a God Who is no respecter of persons! I hold in my hand a lamp that is just as powerful and just as strong as the one the Apostle Paul held in his hand. I hold in my hand a light that shines just as brightly as the lamp that the Apostle Paul held in his hand.

The Word of God is called food in Jeremiah 15:16, "*Thy words were found, and I did eat them....*" God gave Ezekiel His words and told His prophet to eat them. The Word of God is food. Would God give manna from Heaven to one generation and junk food to another generation? Do you mean to tell me that God does not want me to grow in grace as much as He wanted the Apostle Peter to grow in grace? Do you mean to tell me that God wanted those Christians who lived 2,000 years ago to be stronger than God wants you to be? The fundamental, King James Bible people know the Bible better than the non-fundamental, non-King James Bible people do.

One of my favorite stories happened while I was preaching in Casper, Wyoming. The building seated about 700 and was packed with delegates from churches in Wyoming and Montana. While there, I preached separation, soul winning, old-time religion, and an old-fashioned Gospel. A little fellow seated about halfway back heckled me during the whole conference. I preached nine times in one day, and he heckled me all day long.

He would holler out in the service, "Yeah, soul winning, soul winning, soul winning! When do your people get fed?"

I'd preach a while longer, and he'd jeer, "Soul winning, soul winning. I bet you've got a bunch of shallow people."

I'd preach a while longer, and he would comment in a snide way, "We've got deeper-life folks at our church. What kind of baby Christians do you have?"

By 4:00 that day, I had preached about my seventh time, and I had lost all patience with that rascal. I stopped my sermon, walked back to where he was seated, and stood up on the pew beside him. It shocked the entire convention. Loud enough for everyone to hear me, I said, "All day long, you've called my people shallow and your people deep. It's time to put up or shut up! We'll find out who knows the most Bible—an old-time religion, evangelistic, soul-winning, separated, old-fashioned church, or your so-called deeper-life church."

I pointed my finger at him and said, "Buster, I challenge you now to appoint a committee of people to draw up a Bible test. Let that committee give that test to my people and to your people. Let my deacons take the test and your deacons take the test. My Sunday school teachers will take it, and your Sunday school teachers will take it. I will take it, and you will take it! The same folks who drew up the test will grade the tests, and then they'll come back here and let the entire state know once and for all who knows the Bible best—the soul-winning, old-time religion people, or your deeper-life people. Now put up or shut up!"

You listen to me! You get more Bible off the hors d'oeuvres of an old-fashioned, soul-winning church than you do the entrée of a deeper-life church. God would not give one generation manna from Heaven but another generation junk food that is diluted.

The Word of God is called milk in I Peter 2:2. "As newborn babes, desire the sincere milk of the word." Would God give fresh milk to one generation and sour milk to another? I serve a God Who is no respecter of persons. I serve a God Who has given to every generation since this Book was finished the undiluted words of Almighty God.

The Word of God is called the seed in I Peter 1:23. "Being born again, not of corruptible seed, but of incorruptible, by the word of God, which liveth and abideth for ever." James 1:18 says, "Of *his own will begat he us with the word of truth."* This Word is the seed that brings forth the life of a newborn babe. I believe with all my soul that those preaching from a bunch of false bibles are planting corruptible seed. I promise you that when preachers are not using the pure, undiluted, incorruptible words of Almighty God, many tares are going to get born in the family of the Devil rather than people being born into the family of God. Would God give His pure seed to one generation but HIV-infested seed to another generation?

What kind of God do you serve, Bible institute? What kind of God do you serve, NIV toters? You say, "Brother Hyles, those folks who believe several Bibles also believe the seed is incorruptible." Then why does the Bible need changing? Either what they changed from is corruptible or what they are changing to is corruptible or both are corruptible.

In Psalm 119:130, the Word of God is called the source of wisdom. *"The entrance of thy words giveth light; it giveth understanding unto the simple."* In II Timothy 3:15, Apostle Paul reminded Timothy that his grandmother and mother had given him the words of God, *"...able to make thee wise...."* So, the Bible is our source of wisdom. Would God give brilliance to one generation but retardation to another generation? Is not the same wisdom that was available 2,000 years ago available now? Or is God a respecter of persons?

In II Timothy 3:16, the Word of God is called inspired. Would God give word-for-word inspiration to one generation but thought inspiration to another generation? Proverbs 30:5 says, *"Every word of God is pure...."* Would God give all pure words to one generation but impure words to another generation?

The theologians argue, "These men that have translated the Bible down through the years were sinful men." Did you ever read about what kind of men God gave His Word to in the first place? David wasn't known for his sanctity, but God gave him the Psalms. Moses was a murderer, yet God gave him the Pentateuch. Paul had killed Christians, but God gave him the Epistles. Peter cursed, swore, and denied the Lord. I'm saying that if God could take a bunch of imperfect men and reveal to them word for word His Word from Heaven, then He can forever preserve that Word in the pens of imperfect men.

If the Bible needs improving, it isn't perfect. If it now isn't perfect, then God didn't preserve it. If it wasn't perfect and was corrected, then why is there a new one every few months? If it was perfect then and isn't now, then God is a respecter of persons.

I want to remind you that when Paul picked up the Pentateuch to read it, he read words that were as old or older than the Epistles that Paul wrote as we now read them. Nobody seems to doubt that God preserved the words up until the days of the New Testament. If God could preserve for several thousand years the words from Moses to Paul, why couldn't God preserve for 2,000 thousand years the words from Paul to me? If God could not have preserved His words, then He is not omnipotent. If He could have preserved them but didn't, then He is unjust. If we do not have what the first generation had, we have a dull sword, polluted water, a little hammer, smoke with no fire, a dim and dark lamp, junk food, corruptible seed, retarded wisdom, thought inspiration, and partial purity. I'm not sure that I would want to serve a God Who would treat me that way. The truth is, God is no respecter of persons.

Chapter Six

What the Bible Says About Its Preservation

The Bible did not begin when Moses wrote the first five books called the Pentateuch. The Epistles did not begin when Paul sat down and wrote the Epistles. There never was a time when there was no Matthew. There never was a time when there was no Nehemiah. There never was a time when there was no book of Romans. All of the Bible always has been; it never began. Just like the Father and the Son and the Holy Spirit, **the Word of God always was**.

Psalm 119:89 says, *"For ever, O LORD, thy word is settled in heaven."* The verse says, *"is,"* meaning that there is a forever *"is."* The Bible always was, always will be and *is*. God told Moses to tell the people that the "I Am" had sent him. In John 8:58 Jesus said, *"...Before Abraham was, I am."*

• **The Word of God is eternal.** One cannot separate the Word of God from the Trinity. Jesus is called *the Word* in John 1:1, so Jesus cannot be separated from the Word. John 6:63 says, *"It is the spirit that quickeneth; the flesh profiteth nothing: the words that I speak unto you, they are spirit, and they are life."* That verse means that anyone who doesn't live in the Word of God, doesn't know the Word of God, and is not filled with the Word of God cannot be filled with the Holy Spirit. My Bible says that the words and the Spirit are the same. *"...The words that*

I speak unto you, they are spirit…." Don't you tell me that you can be filled with the Holy Spirit but not be filled with the Word of God.

Here is the problem. The words of God were up in Heaven. On earth was a human race that could not live by bread alone, but must have every single one of those words that has always been in Heaven. God had to get those words to us, so He did. But wait a minute, that was several thousand years ago. God gave the Pentateuch through Moses to the people living at that time. What about us today?

The Pentateuch was written several thousand years ago, but no one has the original manuscripts. Some famous theologians love to say, "In the original it says." They don't have the foggiest idea what they are talking about. There's not one single original anywhere nor has there been for years and decades and centuries. No originals exist. God gave His words to the people back in those days through chosen men, but how do we get them now?

David had some of the Bible already but there were no original manuscripts of the Pentateuch of Moses available to David. Yet, David wrote Psalm 12:6 which says, *"The words of the LORD are pure words…."* **"Are?"** That verse means that somehow God had kept those words pure from Moses' time to David's time. If they were pure words, they had to be the same words that God gave to Moses. They had to be the same words that Moses, the penman, wrote as being in the hand of God.

David said, *"The words of the LORD are pure words."* Pure means you can't improve on them. Did you hear what I said, so-called Bible publishers? You can't improve on them. Did you hear what I said, NIV and RSV folks? You cannot improve on *"pure words."*

• **God promised to preserve His words from now on.** Psalm 12:6-7 says, *"The words of the LORD are pure words: as silver tried in a furnace of earth, purified seven times. Thou shalt keep*

them, O LORD, thou shalt preserve them from this generation for
ever." Isaiah 59:20 and 21 says, "And the Redeemer shall come to
Zion, and unto them that turn from transgression in Jacob, saith the
LORD. As for me, this is my covenant with them, saith the LORD;
My spirit that is upon thee, and my words which I have put in thy
mouth, shall not depart out of thy mouth, nor out of the mouth of
thy seed, nor out of the mouth of thy seed's seed, saith the LORD,
from henceforth and for ever."

God is saying, "Isaiah, these words shall linger the rest of
your life, and then they shall linger the rest of your children's
lives. Then they shall be preserved for the rest of your grand-
children's lives. Then they shall be preserved for the rest of
your great-grandchildren's lives, and then they shall be preserved for the rest of your great-great-grandchildren's lives,
and then for the rest of your great-great-great-grandchildren's
lives." God said, "As long as there is a human being on the face
of this earth, My words will be preserved."

From our time and forever back, there always were the
words of God. The words always were in Heaven, and they
always will be in Heaven. There never was a time when the
Word of God did not exist. There never will be a time when
they don't exist. **The Word of God always will be.**

• **The Psalmist says that the law (Genesis-Deuteron-
omy) was preserved.** Psalm 19:7 says, "The law of the LORD is
perfect, converting the soul: the testimony of the LORD is sure, making wise the simple." David had no original manuscripts of the
law; and yet, he said that the law of the Lord is perfect.

• **The Epistles say that the prophets are preserved.**
Romans 1:2 says, "...Which he had promised afore by his prophets
in the **holy scriptures**...." Paul said that the Scriptures were
holy which means "without blame, without a mistake." Paul
said that the copies he had of the prophets (written hundreds
of years before Paul's time) contained the words of God. They
were the "holy Scriptures."

II Peter 3:2 says, "*That ye may be mindful of the words which were spoken before by the **holy prophets,** and of the commandment of us the apostles of the Lord and Saviour.*"

The Psalmist David said that he had the perfect Word of God (the law), and the writers of the Epistles said that they had the perfect prophets.

• **The New Testament says that the entire Old Testament is inspired.** II Timothy 3:16 says, "*All scripture is given by inspiration of God....*" The Scripture they had in Timothy's time was the Old Testament. Paul said that during his time (approximately 4,000 years after Genesis was written) that "*All scripture is given by inspiration of God....*" This verse says *is* not *was.* Paul didn't believe that the prophets were inspired in the originals; he believed that they were inspired then. David didn't believe that the law was inspired in the originals; he believed the law was inspired and perfect then.

People had no original manuscripts in Peter's day, in Paul's day, or in Timothy's day. That means that the Scripture they had then "*is given by inspiration of God.*" The words *is given* are in the Greek durative tense. It is saying that "all Scripture is given and is given and is given." The durative tense means that God keeps on preserving His inspired Scriptures. It does not say that at one time God gave us the Bible. No, it says that at all times God gives us the Bible.

• **Hebrews 1:1 and 2 say that the Old Testament is preserved.** "*God, who at sundry times and in divers manners spake in time past unto the fathers by the prophets, Hath in these last days spoken unto us by his Son....*" Paul is saying that in the Old Testament, God spake unto us by breathed upon holy men, but in the New Testament God has spoken unto us by His perfect Son. The written word that Paul had was just as perfect as the Jesus he had.

• **Revelation 22:18 and 19 say that the entire Bible is preserved.** "*For I testify unto every man that heareth the words of* the prophecy of this book, If any man shall add unto these things, God shall add unto him the plagues that are written in this book: And if any man shall take away from the words of the book of this prophecy, God shall take away his part out of the book of life, and out of the holy city, and from the things which are written in this book." God said that if anyone adds to or takes away from the Book, he will suffer plagues.

You say, "Brother Hyles, you are talking about the book of Revelation." Revelation 20:11 and 12 say, "And I saw a great white throne, and him that sat on it, from whose face the earth and the heaven fled away; and there was found no place for them [This is the end of the Millennium when the unsaved people are raised. They will be judged to determine how hot their Hell will be.] And I saw the dead, small and great, stand before God; and the books were opened: and another book was opened, which is the book of life: and the dead were judged out of those things which were written in **the books,** according to their works."

What are those **books**? These verses say that unsaved people will be judged according to the books. We can conjecture all we want about what these books might be; but if God does everything by His words, then He is going to judge by His words. Sounds to me like **the books** in Revelation are the books of God's Word. To me the logical assumption is that the God Who created the universe by His words and does everything else by His words will judge by His words. Could God judge without His words? No! God has limited Himself to do everything He does by His words.

His Words always were. His words have been breathed into man for this time when man inhabits the earth. His words always will be. I Peter 1:23 says, "Being born again, not of corruptible seed, but of incorruptible by **the word of God, which liveth and abideth for ever.**" Heaven is forever; I am forever; the Bible is forever. We will have in Heaven the eternal words of God that we now have.

Chapter Seven

The Publishing of New Bibles Is Not New

The publishing of new Bibles is nothing new. In fact, I can prove that counterfeit Bibles were being published in Peter's day.

The wise man said, "...*there is no new thing under the sun,*" so don't think for a single moment that our generation has published all the new versions of the Bible. What has been will be, and what goes around comes around.

The Old Testament was older during the New Testament times than the New Testament is now; in fact, the Old Testament was twice as old. The history of man is 6,000 years: 4,000 years before Jesus came to earth and 2,000 years since Jesus came. People changed the Scriptures in Bible times even as people change the Scriptures in our generation. People have been the same all along. They haven't changed. People say, "In these days, more Bibles are being published." No, people have always been changing the Word of God. Satan started changing the Word of God in the Garden of Eden. There's nothing new under the sun.

In II Peter, not only did the Apostle Peter warn Christians about people who were changing the Scriptures, but he also warned them of the most unbelievable judgment that would be pronounced on those who changed the Scriptures.

II Peter 1:16 says, *"For we have not followed cunningly devised fables."* That word *fables* means "fiction." Peter was saying, "These words are not fiction." I wonder why he said that? I have an idea that there were folks in those days who didn't believe Jonah was swallowed by the whale. In those days there were folks who didn't believe the whole earth was flooded or that Elijah prayed down fire from Heaven. There have always been people who didn't believe the Word of God, and there have always been fundamentalists who believe the Word of God. There have always been liberals who change the Word of God, infidels who compromise the Word of God, and pussy-footers who are afraid to preach the Word of God. There has been no real change.

Peter said, *"...we have not followed cunningly devised fables."* There is no crowd more cunning or deceptive than the new-Bible-printing crowd. Why? The publishers say that they're trying to make the Bible easier for the average person to understand, but the truth is that they are trying to make a buck. The Bible has been the most popular seller for many years in America. These cunning publishers are taking that popular seller and reprinting it in many forms, so they can make more money. In II Peter 1:16, Peter is warning the Christians about these people who *cunningly devised fables.*

Verse 16 continues, *"...when we made known unto you the power and coming of our Lord Jesus Christ, but were eyewitnesses of his majesty."* Peter said, "I saw Jesus. I walked with Him. I saw Jesus walk on the water. I saw Him do many good things. I heard Him preach. I saw Him feed the five thousand. I saw Him in the upper room. I was there when He washed the disciples' feet. I saw Him heal the sick and raise the dead. I'm an eyewitness." That eye-witness account is pretty good, isn't it? How would you like to know someone who saw Jesus?

Verse 17 states, *"For he received from God the Father honour and glory, when there came such a voice to him from the excellent* glory, *This is my beloved Son, in whom I am well pleased.*" Peter said, "I saw Jesus, but that isn't all. At the baptism of Jesus, I heard the voice of God say, '…*This is my beloved Son, in whom I am well pleased.*' I saw Jesus, and I heard God the Father."

Verse 18 says, "*And this voice which came from heaven we heard, when we were with him in the holy mount.*" Peter explained, "I heard that same voice at the transfiguration when Jesus and James and John and I went up to the top of the mountain where we met with Elijah and Moses at the transfiguration." Peter saw Jesus, heard the voice of God the Father at His Son's baptism, and heard that same voice again at the transfiguration. Peter saw Elijah, Moses, and Jesus in His glorified body.

In verse 14 Peter said, "*Knowing that shortly I must put off this my tabernacle,* [Peter said, 'I've got to die,'] *even as our Lord Jesus Christ hath shewed me.*" Peter also said, "Jesus taught me." Notice the privileges Peter had. Wouldn't you have loved to have seen Jesus when He was here on earth? Wouldn't you have loved to hear that voice from Heaven saying, "*This is my beloved Son, in whom I am well pleased*"? Wouldn't you have loved to have heard the voice of God on the mount of transfiguration? Wouldn't you have loved to have seen Elijah and Moses? Wouldn't you have loved to have been taught by Jesus Himself? Peter said, "I got to do all of that."

Notice something very interesting in verse 19 which says, "*We have also a more sure word of prophecy….*" What a Scripture! What is Peter saying? Peter didn't have his epistle. He didn't have Romans, I or II Corinthians, Galatians, Ephesians, Philippians, Colossians, I or II Timothy, I or II Thessalonians, Timothy, Titus, Hebrews, James, I or II Peter, I, II, or III John, Jude, or Revelation. He didn't have any of those books. Peter was saying, "To read the Bible is better than seeing Jesus personally on earth. To have this Book is better than hearing the voice of God speak over the Jordan River. To have this Book is better than hearing the voice of God at the transfiguration. To have this Book is better than being taught by Jesus Himself." Peter was saying that you and I have a better proof of the Gospel in the Bible than he had by seeing the Lord Jesus Christ Himself. He said, *"We have also a more sure word of prophecy."*

Consider the account of the rich man and Lazarus. Lazarus was a beggar who sat at the rich man's table begging for the crumbs that would fall. Both the rich man and Lazarus died. In Hell, the rich man lifted up his eyes and saw Abraham with Lazarus. The rich man cried out to God in Luke 16:27-31, *"...I pray thee therefore, father, that thou wouldest send him to my father's house: For I have five brethren; that he may testify unto them, lest they also come into this place of torment. Abraham saith unto him, They have Moses and the prophets;* [Genesis-Deuteronomy and the books written by the prophets] *let them hear them. And he said, Nay, father Abraham: but if one went unto them from the dead, they will repent. And he said unto him, If they hear not Moses and the prophets, neither will they be persuaded, though one rose from the dead."*

Someone should tell Oral Roberts about those verses. There is more power in preaching the Bible than in the healing of cancer or in making the cripple to walk. There is more power in preaching God's Word. Moses and the prophets is all that the people in Luke 16 had. Today's Christians now have all of God's Word, the total revelation. The Bible is better than a healing service. It is better than a so-called miracle-working services.

If I had my choice between preaching the Bible next Sunday morning or going to the cemetery to raise somebody from the dead and letting him tell people what he had seen, I'd leave that person in the grave, so I could preach the Book! The answer is in the Book. The answer is not in somebody's testimony. The answer is in the Book. The answer is not in somebody's miracle. The answer is in God's Word!

Abraham said that the Bible is more powerful than the testimony of a person raised from the dead. Peter was somebody who had the power of God, yet Peter said the Bible is more powerful than the testimony of someone who saw Jesus on earth, who heard the voice of God as Jesus was baptized, who heard the voice of God on the mount of transfiguration, and who saw and talked to Moses and Elijah. Peter said God's Word will do more to get people saved and has more power than all those events put together. What a passage!

II Peter 1:20 says, *"Knowing this first, that no prophecy of the scripture is of any private interpretation."* What is this verse saying? Peter is saying that man has nothing to do with it. He is saying that this Book is the Book of God's words and not man's words. He's saying that God did not give man the thought and man put down the thought in his own words. He's saying that the Bible has nothing to do with an individual.

What is it then? Peter explains in verse 21. *"For the prophecy came not in old time by the will of man: but holy men of God spake as they were moved by the Holy Ghost."* That word, *holy,* doesn't mean "perfect" men. It means "chosen or set apart." As I mentioned in chapter three, these were men whom God had chosen and set apart.

So, Peter said, "I saw it. I heard the voice of God in the Jordan River. I heard the voice of God on the mount of transfiguration. I talked to Moses and Elijah. Jesus taught me Himself. I was in the classroom when Jesus was the professor, but I've got something better now. I have the Word of God."

Let's look at II Peter 1:19 again, *"We have also a **more sure** word of prophecy...."* Peter said that the Word of God is **more sure** than seeing Jesus, **more sure** than hearing the voice of God when Jesus was baptized, **more sure** than hearing the voice of God on the mount of transfiguration, **more sure** than seeing Jesus' glorified body on that mount, **more sure** than seeing Elijah, and **more sure** than seeing Moses.

Christians today have something better! How much better? Verse 19 continues, "...*whereunto ye do well that ye take heed, as unto a light that shineth in a dark place, until the day dawn, and the day star arise in your hearts.*" Peter said that it was wonderful to hear the voice of God at the Jordan River and see to Jesus teach, heal, preach, and be baptized. He said going to the mount of transfiguration and hearing again the same voice of God, and seeing Moses and Elijah was like a light shining in darkness, but Peter said that when God's Book came along, the sun came up!

What does Peter mean? Peter was saying that a person had to be at the Jordan River to hear the voice of God that day, but this Book is heard around the world. Peter was saying that seeing Jesus, hearing the voice of God, being on the mount of transfiguration, and seeing Elijah and Moses is insignificant as a flashlight in the darkness compared to the Bible which is compared to the sunrise of a new day.

The Bible says in John 1:5, "*And the light shineth in darkness...*" We have the Bible! To live in our generation is better than living when Jesus was on earth, just as the sunshine of a new day is better than a flashlight shining at midnight. What a day to live in!

Peter was saying, "You have it. You have the Bible, "*...a more sure word of prophecy....*"

II Peter 2:1 introduces the scholars of Peter's day. "*But there were false prophets also among the people, even as there shall be false teachers among you, who privily shall bring in damnable heresies....*" The word *heresies* means "substitutions." Peter was saying in II Peter 1:19 that we have "*a more sure word of prophecy,*" but the false prophets will come in and bring substitutions to that Book of sure words. This was happening 2,000 years ago during the first century.

They had so-called Bible publishers in those days. Notice

what Peter called these "substitution folks"; he called them
"false teachers." Those rascals who edited and published the
New King James Bible are false teachers. Those rascals who
publish the NIV Bible are false teachers, as are those birds who
put out the *New American Standard Bible.* Peter taught that we
have *"a more sure word of prophecy,"* but he also warned that
some false prophets and some false teachers are coming who
will substitute words in the Bible.

II Peter 2:1 says, *"...who privily shall bring in damnable heresies, even denying the Lord...."* That verse states exactly what
happened in the *American Standard Version.* Any time man
tries to improve on what God does, he is exalting himself.
When you exalt yourself, you bring down the Saviour. Those
men have denied the Lord.

II Peter 2:2 says, *"And many shall follow their pernicious
ways...."* Peter was saying that many will read the New
Scofield and the NIV of their day.

Verse 2 continues, *"...by reason of whom the way of truth
shall be evil spoken of."* Just as these false teachers were speaking evil in Peter's day, liberal professors in their classrooms are
speaking evil of fundamental "ignoramuses." They teach,
"Hyles is no scholar." No, I wouldn't pass as a scholar by ignorant men. As a matter of fact, I don't want Bible rejecters calling me a scholar. I don't want people who change the Book
calling me a scholar.

Notice the word *"evil,"* in verse 2. Sin and evil do not have
the same meaning. *Sin* is the transgression of God's law; *evil* is
a transgression of God's law that hurts people. I knew the men
who edited and published the *New King James Version.* I was
invited to be on the overview committee of that perversion of
the Bible. Those men did evil; they hurt people by taking away
the words of God.

You say, "Brother Hyles, I met one of those men, and he
was one of the nicest men I've ever met." Evil people usually

are the nicest people. The nicest preachers you'll ever meet are liberal preachers. They never have to get angry at anything. I don't care how sweet the editors are; if they change the Bible, they are as rotten as the Devil himself. Not only are they false teachers and false prophets, they are evil men. It is interesting that there were evil false teachers changing the Bible in Peter's day.

II Peter 2:3 explains why these false prophets were making these changes. *"And through covetousness shall they with feigned words* [made up words] *make merchandise of you...."* These people were changing the Bible to sell the new ones. Two thousand years ago those people took Moses and the prophets (all of the Bible that they had) and substituted other words for the words of God. God said they were false teachers and false prophets trying to make a dollar.

If these Bible publishers want to prove their sincerity, let them print these Bibles free of charge and scatter them around the world. If so-called Christian bookstores are so interested in getting out the Word of God, why don't they sell the books at cost, and not make a profit?

Publishing new Bibles has been going on for 2,000 years, so there is nothing new under the sun. Peter warned the people, "Watch it, folks. We saw Jesus, but we've got something better. We heard the voice of God, but we have something better. We went to the mount of transfiguration, but we have something better. We were taught by Jesus, but we have something better—*'a more sure word of prophecy,'* God's Book. Now because this book is better, some people are trying to change it. They are evil people, who are trying to make merchandise."

Peter also warned them about the punishment of these evil men in verse 4 which says, *"For if God spared not the angels that sinned, but cast them down to hell, and delivered them into chains of darkness, to be reserved unto judgment."* God is saying these men will be judged. If God cast angels out of Heaven into everlasting torment (Matthew 25:41), God will also do the same to these wicked men. Peter said that the same God Who kicked angels out of Heaven because they had sinned, and the same God Who kicked Lucifer out of Heaven and consigned Lucifer and his angels to Hell forever is going to judge these evil men—these false teachers who change God's Word.

As we can see, the publishing of new Bibles is not new. It began with Satan when He changed God's Word in Genesis 3; it continued through Peter's day and is rampant in our generation.

I would rather be the owner of a house of prostitution when I stand before God than somebody who said, "I can tell you better what God said than He can tell you." If the Bible needs changing, one time ought to be enough. Publishing houses, why do you print different ones and improve the improvement and improve the improvement? The truth is, you're not! You're deteriorating the better, which was deteriorating the best.

II Peter 2:6 says, *"And turning the cities of Sodom and Gomorrah into ashes."* God is saying that the same God Who kicked the angels out of Heaven is going to judge these fellows. The same God Who sent the flood on the earth will judge these rascals, too. The same God Who sent fire on Sodom and Gomorrah said that these fellows are as bad as those homosexuals in Sodom.

Someone might say, "Brother Hyles, you seem angry about these new versions." Of course, I am! Somebody has said my God's words need improving. If I were the Devil, I certainly would know the power of the Book. Jesus used it against the Devil. If I were the Devil, the first thing I'd try to do is change the Book. By the way that is the first thing he did try in Genesis chapter three. From that day until this, the Book has been the most powerful instrument in the work of God ever known to mankind.

Shall I have a dead person come and speak? No, I'll just preach the Book. Shall I have Peter come and tell what Jesus looked like? No, I'll just preach the Book. Shall I have Peter, James, and John come and recount the transfiguration? No, I'll just preach the Book. Shall I have them tell us what the voice of God sounded like when Jesus got baptized in the Jordan River? No, I'll just preach the Book. God has provided today's Christian with *a more sure word of prophecy.*

Chapter Eight

The Author of the New Versions

In the Bible, Satan makes three appearances—in Genesis 3, in Job 1, and in Matthew 4. Each of those times Satan appears to accuse. In Genesis 3, the Devil comes to accuse God to man. He says to Adam and Eve, "God is not telling you the truth." In Job 1, Satan accuses man to God. In Matthew 4, Satan accuses the Saviour, the God-man, in the time of temptation. In every appearance, Satan's accusations involved the Word of God.

Genesis 2:8-9 says, "*And the* LORD *God planted a garden eastward in Eden; and there he put the man whom he had formed. And out of the ground made the* LORD *God to grow every tree that is pleasant to the sight, and good for food; the tree of life also in the midst of the garden, and the tree of knowledge of good and evil.*"

Three different divisions are presented in these verses:

(1) Every tree in the garden pleasant to the sight and good for food.

(2) In the midst of the garden is the tree of life.

(3) There is also the tree of the knowledge of good and evil.

Notice the Bible does not say that the tree of the knowledge of good and evil was in the garden. I personally believe that the tree of the knowledge of good and evil was in Eden, but not *in* the Garden of Eden. I believe that Adam and Eve had to go outside of the garden to get to that tree.

Genesis 2:15-17 says, "*And the* LORD *God took the man, and put him into the garden of Eden to dress it and to keep it. And the* LORD *God commanded the man, saying, Of every tree in the garden thou mayest freely eat: But of the tree of the knowledge of good and evil, thou shalt not eat of it: For in the day that thou eatest thereof, thou shalt surely die.*"

Genesis 3:1 continues, "*Now the serpent was more subtil than any beast of the field which the* LORD *God had made. And he said unto the woman, Yea, hath God said, Ye shall not eat of every tree of the garden?*" Did God say, "*ye shall not eat of every tree of the garden*"? No! He said that Adam and Eve could eat of every tree of the garden. The Devil added one word and changed the entire meaning of God's words. Satan is adding to the Word of God which is exactly what the *Revised Standard Version* does and the NIV, the ASV, and the other modern versions of the Bible are doing. These versions add to the Word of God which changes the meaning.

Genesis 3:2-3 says, "*And the woman said unto the serpent, We may eat of the fruit of the trees of the garden: But of the fruit of the tree which is in the midst of the garden, God hath said, Ye shall not eat of it….*" Is that what God said? The tree in the midst of the garden was the tree of life. The tree of which God forbade Adam and Eve to eat was the tree of the knowledge of good and evil. Here, Eve also changed the Bible.

Eve continues in verse 3, "*…Ye shall not eat of it neither shall ye touch it….*" God did not say that Adam and Eve could not touch the tree. God said, "*Ye shall not eat of it.*" Eve was fiddling with the Word of God. Just like Eve, a bunch of seminary professors and publishers are fiddling with the Word of God.

Genesis 3:4 says, "*And the serpent said unto the woman, Ye shall not surely die.*" Compare what the serpent said in Genesis 3:2 to what God said in Genesis 2:17 which says, "*…for in the* *day that thou eatest thereof thou shalt surely die."* The Devil is calling God a liar! **The Devil is saying that the Word of God is not literal.** Our evangelical "friends" hold this same position. They say, "We believe in the inspiration of the Scriptures, but we don't believe in the literal interpretation of the Bible. Those dragons in Revelation are not really dragons." If God didn't mean what He said, then why didn't God say what He meant? The Devil told Eve not to believe a literal interpretation of the Bible.

Recently, I read a magazine article entitled, "Is the Bible True?" The article said that Moses was a figment of the imagination of the Jewish people and that Abraham and Moses were characters invented by the Jewish people. Then the article said, "There are those literalists of Bible interpretation." If the Bible is not literal, how in the world do you know what it means? God always means what He says unless God says He doesn't mean what He says. If God says, "The kingdom of heaven is likened to...," that statement is literal. If God says, "As a man goes into a far country...," that statement is not literal.

The Devil says that the Bible is not literal. Yes, it is! Satan is calling God a liar. Every stinking one of those self-styled scholars who spend their lives changing the Bible rather than spreading the Bible is calling Almighty God a liar.

The time has come for Christians to say what they believe. If you don't believe we have a Bible, then say it! If you believe we have a Bible, then say it! Those who change the King James Bible are inspired by the one who changed the Bible the first time in Genesis.

First the Devil said, "God has said that you cannot eat of every tree in the garden." Then the Devil added, "You are not going to die."

The Devil continues talking to Eve in Genesis 3:5. *"...For God doth know that in the day ye eat thereof, then your eyes shall* be opened, and ye shall be as gods, knowing good and evil." The Devil is now telling Eve, "If you will listen to me, you can have your own interpretation of the Bible." That's exactly what the Devil wants! If there are ten million Christians in America, the Devil wants ten million different ideas of what the Bible is.

The Devil is not trying to get you to endorse the NIV. He would just as soon have you endorse the *Reader's Digest Condensed Version* or the *Douay Version* or any other version as long as you leave the King James Bible.

There was a day when a Christian had two choices: the *American Standard* or the King James Bible. Then came the RSV, giving a person two places to escape the King James Bible. Then came the NIV, giving a person three places to escape the King James Bible. Then came the *New King James Bible*, giving people four places to escape the King James Bible. And now there are hundreds of versions, giving people hundreds of places to escape the King James Bible. I am also including the children's Bibles. A children's Bible that is not exactly the King James text is one of the Devil's bibles. Some say, "How do you expect children to understand the Bible?" My mama helped me understand the King James Bible quite well. The trouble with the average person is not that he can't understand the Bible; his trouble is that he does not read the Bible.

First, the Devil added to the Bible. Next, he called God a liar and made the Bible not literal. Then he said, "Write your own Bible. You will be as gods." That means that Adam and Eve could decide for themselves what was good and bad. That is exactly what the Devil desires. The Devil does not want you to go off to a state university and have them direct you to another Bible. He wants you to go there and have them direct you to believe what you want to believe. We do not have one cotton-picking right to believe what *we* want to believe. We only have the right to believe what the God of this universe believes. That is what Isaiah 53:6 means when it says, "*All we like sheep have gone astray; we have turned every one to his own way....*" The Devil wants to get you away from the King James Bible, and he doesn't care which way you go.

Look at the excuses Adam and Eve made to God. Genesis 3:8-13 says, "*And they heard the voice of the LORD God walking in the garden in the cool of the day: and Adam and his wife hid themselves from the presence of the LORD God amongst the trees of the garden. And the LORD God called unto Adam, and said unto him, Where art thou? And he said, I heard thy voice in the garden, and I was afraid, because I was naked; and I hid myself. And he said, Who told thee that thou wast naked? Hast thou eaten of the tree, whereof I commanded thee that thou shouldest not eat? And the man said, The woman whom thou gavest to be with me, she gave me of the tree, and I did eat. And the LORD God said unto the woman, What is this that thou hast done? And the woman said, The serpent beguiled me, and I did eat.*"

Notice whom Adam and Eve blamed. Eve blamed the serpent. Adam blamed Eve. Adam also blamed God by saying, "*...the woman whom **thou** gavest to be with me....*" Adam was saying, "If You had not given me that woman, I still would not have eaten of that fruit. You gave me that woman. It's Your fault." The sin of the Garden of Eden was that Adam and Eve and the Devil had a new version of the Bible.

The sin of the Garden of Eden was changing the Bible. During the first appearance of the Devil, he fiddled with the Word of God.

The next time the Devil appears is in Job 1:6-10 which says, "*Now there was a day when the sons of God came to present themselves before the LORD and Satan came also among them. And the LORD said unto Satan, Whence comest thou? Then Satan answered the LORD, From going to and fro in the earth, and from walking up and down in it. And the LORD said unto Satan, Hast thou considered my servant Job, that there is none like him in the* earth, a perfect and an upright man, one that feareth God, and escheweth evil? Then Satan answered the LORD, and said, Doth Job fear God for nought? Hast not thou not made a hedge about him...." The Devil doubted the Word of God.

The third appearance of the Devil was at the temptation of our Lord. Matthew 4:5-6 says, "*Then the devil taketh him up into the holy city, and setteth him on a pinnacle of the temple, And saith unto him, If thou be the son of God, cast thyself down: for it is written, He shall give his angels charge* **concerning** *thee: and in their hands they shall bear thee up, lest* **at any time** *thou dash thy foot against a stone.*" The Devil is supposedly quoting Psalm 91:11 when he uses the word *concerning*.

Psalm 91:11 and 12 say, "*For he shall give his angels charge* **over** *thee,* **to keep thee in all thy ways***. They shall bear thee up in their hands, lest thou dash thy foot against a stone.*" Satan changes the Word of God. God said, "*over.*" Satan used the word, "concerning." God said, "*They shall bear thee up in their hand.*" Satan said, "In their hands, they shall bear thee up." The Devil also takes away the words "*and keep thee in all thy ways.*" The Devil instead adds the words, "at any time." This is the Devil giving us yet another version of the Bible. Some say, "Brother Hyles, it's the same meaning." Then they believe in thought inspiration or meaning inspiration. The Bible doesn't say, "Man shall live by **every thought** or **every meaning**." The Bible says, "*every word.*"

Don't you think that the Devil knew Psalm 91:11 and 12? As Satan was God's right-hand deputy in Heaven, he knew God and the Word of God. Satan had free access to the Word of God in Heaven. The Devil knew these verses and changed them. That is what he has been doing for 6,000 years! Let the Devil go back to Hell where he belongs and let him take his professors with him.

In Psalm 91:11 and 12, Satan omitted seven words, changed one word, added three words, and rearranged a sentence. My Bible says that those who take away from the words of the prophecy of God will have the plagues of Revelation added unto them, and a curse will be placed on them. This means the Devil, but it also applies to liberal seminary professors. It means anybody! I am sick and tired of theologians who hide behind the guise of scholarship when it is nothing more than deceit. Good, godly Christians across America are being deceived by a bunch of self-styled, so-called scholars who say they know God's Word better than God does. Leave the Bible alone! Get on a street corner and preach it!

In all three appearances of the Devil, he has taken away, added to, changed, rearranged, and doubted the Word of God. Who do you think is the real author of the new versions?

Theologians will say, "Dr. Hyles, the Bible was handed down from generation to generation, and some of the words are going to change." Jeremiah 36:4 says, *"Then Jeremiah called Baruch the son of Neriah: and Baruch wrote from the mouth of Jeremiah all the words of the LORD which he had spoken unto him, upon a roll of a book."* This verse in Jeremiah was recorded by Baruch. God gave this verse to Jeremiah. God gave the words to Jeremiah who gave the words to Baruch, and we still have all the words of the Lord.

Who wrote the book of Romans? Romans 16:22 says, *"I Tertius, who wrote this epistle, salute you in the Lord."* This verse says Tertius wrote Romans, but God gave the book of Romans to Paul. So the Word of God can go from God to man to another man and still be the very words that God gave.

Every single word of God has been preserved in the King James Bible, the only Bible! All the other versions that add to, take away, or change the King James Bible are satanically inspired. The NIV, the ASV, the NASV, the *Reader's Digest Condensed Version*, the RSV, the *Living Bible*, and all other so-called Bibles are inspired by the Devil. All the changes in the Bible come from the fellow who changed God's words in the first place. Every time the Devil has reared his ugly head, he has attacked the Bible and the words of God. Satan is the real author of the new versions.

Chapter Nine

The Ways the Devil Attacks the Bible

In Psalm 119, the Bible is referred to as *law, statutes, judgments, commandments*, etc. Many terms are used for the Bible. Deuteronomy 4:1 and 2 say, "*Now therefore hearken, O Israel unto the statutes and unto the judgments, which I teach you, for to do them, that ye may live, and go in and possess the land which the LORD God of your fathers giveth you. Ye shall not add unto the word which I command you, neither shall ye diminish ought from it, that ye may keep the commandments of the LORD your God which I command you.*"

Moses was saying, "How can you keep the commandments of God if you don't have a clear commandment? Do not add to the Word and do not diminish the Word so you will be able to keep the commandments of God." In other words, if you add to or diminish a commandment, the commandment will not be clear, and you won't know what the commandment of God is. God's Word is very clear when it says that man is not supposed to add to the Words of God nor diminish the Words of God. God's Word is also very clear about the punishment of those that add to or diminish the Words of God.

Revelation 22:18, 19, "*For if I testify unto every man that heareth the words of the prophecy of this book, If any man shall add unto these things, God shall add unto him the plagues that are writ-*

ten in this book: And if any man shall take away from the words of the book of this prophecy, God shall take away his part out of the book of life, and out of the holy city, and from the things which are written in this book."

This Book of Life is not just a book of names. The Book of Life is a book of many sections with one section being the book of names. The Bible says that our names were written in the Book of Life from the foundation of the world.

Not only is a saved person's name written in the Book of Life, but likewise, a saved person's works are written in the Book of Life, and his rewards are written in the Book of Life. When the Bible says, *"...God will take away his part out of the book of life...,"* the verse does not mean his name will be scratched out of the Book of Life. It is not saying if you take away from this Book, God will take away your name from the Book of Life. It says He'll take away *"his part"* and *"part...of the holy city."* What does that mean? Very simply, it means that if a person takes away from the Bible, God will take away some of the rewards that person would have received. Some of the things that are written in the Book of Life for which he would have been rewarded will be taken away. This is one place where the Bible talks about losing rewards.

When God says that He will take away a person's part out of the holy city, it simply means that person will not enjoy Heaven as much as he would have. This verse is not saying that God removes anybody's name from the Book of Life. That would be contrary to the Bible's teachings that when a person gets saved, he cannot lose his salvation.

If the folks at these publishing companies who published the dirty, wicked NIV Bible are saved, (and I'm not saying they're not saved), then God has taken away some of their rewards out of the Book of Life. Also, God has taken away some of their enjoyment of Heaven out of the Book of Life because they have taken away from His Book.

It's a serious indictment for anyone to change or tamper with the Word of God. God says, "If you tamper with My Record, then I'll tamper with yours. You change My Book, and I'll change your part in the book up here. You change My Book down there, and I'll change your book up here. You take away My words down there, and I'll take away your rewards up here in Heaven." God gives a special warning to those who add to or take away from His Book.

The Devil attacks (changes) the Word of God in several ways.

1. The Devil adds to the Words of God. Deuteronomy 4:2 says, "*Ye shall not add unto the word which I command you.*" I'm going to mention some of these so-called bibles to show that these "bibles" are committing the sin God is mentioning in this verse.

For instance, the *Catholic Bible* has added the Apocryphal books between the Old and New Testament. The Mormons have the *Book of Mormon* plus the Bible. The Catholics and the Mormons say that the Bible is okay, but they have added to the Bible.

Proverbs 30:5 says, "*...he is a shield unto them that put their trust in him.* **Add thou not** *unto his words, lest he reprove thee, and* **thou be found a liar**." Publishers of these so-called new Bibles, you are liars! Anybody that adds to the Word of God is a liar.

According the Proverbs 30:5, the Catholic "Bible" and the Book of Mormon are not Bibles at all because these books **added to** the Words of God.

2. The Devil subtracts from the Words of God. Revelation 22:19 says, "*And if any man shall* **take away** *from the words of this book of this prophecy, God shall take away his part out of the book of life, and out of the holy city....*"

The *Reader's Digest Condensed Version* is an example of subtracting from the Bible. That means if anybody in Reader's Digest is saved (which I doubt) and anybody who worked on that condensed Bible is saved, he took away from the words of God. He condensed the words of God. My Bible says if the person is saved, some of his rewards will be taken out of the Book of Life. Likewise, he will not enjoy Heaven because some of the enjoyment he would have had in Heaven will likewise be taken out of the Book of Life. This reference also includes the ASV, NASV, RSV, NIV and all other versions that "*take away*" from the Words of God.

3. The Devil diminishes the Word of God. Deuteronomy 4:2, "*Ye shall not add unto the word which I command you, neither shall ye **diminish** ought from it, that ye may keep the commandments of the LORD your God which I command you.*"

Deuteronomy 12:32 states, "*What thing soever I command you, observe to do it: thou shalt not add thereto, nor **diminish** from it.*"

The word, **diminish**, does not mean "takes away some of the words." The word, *diminish*, is an interesting word which means, "makes simpler in order to clarify."

Did you know the Devil is working awfully hard on children's Bibles these days? The publishers say, "We want to put the Bible in the language a child can understand." The publishers better keep it in the language in which God gave it!

To **add to** means "to add some of your own words to the Bible." To **take away** means "to take away part of the Bible," but to **diminish** means "to change some of the Bible to make it simpler and easier to understand." The Bible is not hard to understand. On the contrary, this Book is easy for anyone to understand—even children.

God said, "I don't want you adding anything to My Book; I don't want you taking anything away from My Book; and I don't want you making anything simpler in My Book. I gave you the Words; don't tamper with Them. Leave Them just like they are and don't meddle with Them."

4. The Devil steals the words of God. Jeremiah 23:30-32, "*Therefore, behold, I am against the prophets, saith the* LORD, *that steal my words every one from his neighbour. Behold, I am against the prophets, saith the* LORD, *that use their tongues, and say, He saith. Behold, I am against them that prophesy false dreams....*"

What were these prophets doing? They were having dreams and saying those dreams were the Words of the Lord. They were having prophecies and saying those prophecies were the words of the Lord. They were having words of knowledge and saying those words of knowledge were the words of the Lord. They were having visions and saying those visions were the words of the Lord.

God doesn't tell you what to do through visions; God tells you what to do through His Book. God doesn't tell you what to do because you had a dream; God tells you what to do through His Book. It's time Christians realized that the way you find the will of God is through the Book!

These prophets in Jeremiah's time were **stealing** the Word of God from the people because they were saying "this vision." In 599 B.C., these "charismatic evangelists" were saying, "I have a word of knowledge."

I say, "Open the Bible, and shut your big, fat, money-grabbing mouth!"

They will say, "I have a word from the Lord," but it may be caused by too many onions on their hamburgers last night. Well, I've got a whole Book of Words from the Lord, and mine is caused by divine revelation as God spoke to holy men of old. A person may **guess** that he has the words of the Lord, but it is his discernment that decides. I don't have to guess; I **know** I have the Words of the Lord. So forget your visions and words of knowledge; open the Book and preach it!

I'm saying that a person who stands up and preaches on the word of knowledge he got from God is **stealing** the Word of God from you. If he stands up and tells you about a vision he had, he's **stealing** the Word of God from you. If he stands up and tells you about a dream he had, he's **stealing** the Word of God from you. If he stands up and tells you about a word of prophecy he had, he's **stealing** the Word of God from you.

The Devil attacks the Bible by **adding to, taking away, diminishing,** and **stealing** the Words of God. The *Book of Mormon* and the *Catholic Bible* add to the words of God. The *Reader's Digest Condensed Version* takes away from the words of God. The children's Bibles and the NIV diminish the words of God. The publishers who say, "We'll give you a Bible that's easier to understand," are giving us another bible on which they can make a profit. The RSV is a bible that takes away and diminishes the Words of God.

5. The Devil perverts or changes the words of the Lord. Jeremiah 23:35, 36, *"Thus shall ye say every one to his neighbour, and every one to his brother, What hath the LORD answered? and, What hath the LORD spoken? And the burden of the LORD shall ye mention no more: for every man's word shall be his burden; for ye have perverted the words of the living God...."* That word, *perverted*, means **"to change"** the words. What is a perversion? A man having sex with a man is a perversion because that is not natural. When a person changes the Words of God, it is a perversion. The NIV, the *New King James,* and the *New Scofield* all **change** the Words of God. They **pervert** the Words of God, and they are of the Devil.

6. The Devil adds "like" words. When Jeremiah was in jail, God said to him, "I want you to write down the Words I'm going to give you." Jeremiah could not write the words because he was in prison, so he called for Baruch, a scribe.

Jeremiah said to Baruch, "God is giving me some words, and I want to dictate them to you." Jeremiah did not write these words. God gave them to Jeremiah, but Baruch transcribed them. These words were preserved from God to

Jeremiah to this scribe Baruch. After Baruch took down these words, Jeremiah said to Baruch, "I can't go to the house of God to read those words because I'm in jail. Baruch, you go for me."

Baruch went to the house of God and read the words he transcribed for Jeremiah. Some princes of King Jehoiakim heard about it and sent for Baruch. Baruch came to the house of the princes and read the words of God in their presence. The princes took from Baruch the roll on which the words of God were written and went to the court of the king. When Jehudi read three or four pages to the king, Jehoiakim ripped up the pages and threw them in the fire, thereby destroying the words of God.

Jeremiah 36:27 says, *"Then the word of the LORD came to Jeremiah, after that the king had burned the roll, and the words which Baruch wrote at the mouth of Jeremiah, saying, Take again another roll, and write in it all the former words that were in the first roll."* You can't destroy the Word of God, King Jehoiakim! The Word of God liveth forever!

Jeremiah 36:32 says, *"Then took Jeremiah another roll, and gave it to Baruch the scribe, the son of Neriah; who wrote therein from the mouth of Jeremiah all the words of the book which Jehoiakim king of Judah had burned in the fire: and there were added besides unto them many **like words**."* That's a mistake. **Like** words were added. Another word for *like words* is "synonyms." This is what happened in the first *Amplified Bible*. The authors of the *Amplified Bible* do not claim it's a Bible; they say it's just a book of synonyms.

The Devil is very cunning in his attack on the Bible. Not only does he add to, take away, diminish, steal, and pervert the words of God; he adds **like** words.

The Words of God are manifested in two ways—in print and in the flesh. The same people who will change one will change the other. The same person who changes the written Word will also say, "Jesus is not virgin born." If they'll change, pervert, add to, diminish, take away, and steal the **written** Word, sooner or later they will do the same thing to the **Living** Word.

We have to watch for the shrewd methods of Satan. He will say, "Look, you could understand it better if I added a bit."

God says, "Satan's a liar."

"Okay," the Devil says. "You might understand better if I took away part of it; there's too much of it. Let's take away the *begats*, and *begottens*, and all the kings, and all the genealogies, and let's just prune it down."

God says, "No! Man has to have **every** word.

The Devil then says, "I'll add to; if that doesn't work, I'll take away; and if that doesn't work, I'll diminish. I'll say, 'It's hard to understand,' and I'll make the words easier and clarify it. If that doesn't work, I'll steal the words. I'll make a preacher say, 'I've just had a vision, and God spoke to me.' If that doesn't work, I'll pervert the words."

God warns, "You look out for any crowd that does that."

The battle is for the Bible. People say, "Brother Hyles, why didn't you take this stand 35 or 40 years ago?" Basically 35 or 40 years ago, the only Bibles available were the ASV, the King James, and the RSV. Everybody knew the RSV was put out by the National Council of Churches. You could hardly find a Bible institute or a Bible college that used anything but the King James Bible and believed it as the Word of God.

Do you know who has added to, taken away, diminished, stolen, and perverted the Words of God? Liberal professors in colleges and seminaries. Most of them were men called to preach the Gospel, but they decided to become theologians. I thank God that the Bible professors at Hyles-Anderson College are preachers of the Bible.

Some may say, "That's not very scholarly." Look, Mr. Liberal Professor, God says it's not scholarly when you add to His Book, when you take from His Book, when you diminish

His Book, when you steal His Book, or when you pervert His Book. God says that it is not good. You will be surprised when you get to Heaven. Your students will see your rewards taken away. Then while some of these "ignorant" fundamental Baptists who run around screaming about the Bible are living on Mansion Row, Mr. Liberal Professor, you'll be living out in a shack in shanty town—if you get there at all.

Chapter Ten

Unprinted False Versions of the Bible

A lot of to-do is made about the NIV and should be; it's not Bible. The *New King James* is not Bible. The *New Scofield* is not Bible. The *American Standard* and the *New American Standard* are not Bibles. The *Revised Standard Version* is not Bible. The *Reader's Digest Condensed Version* is not Bible. In addition to these versions, there are many other versions that are not in print.

Anyone who knows the Bible knows that the book of Jeremiah deals with the Babylonian captivity. God is about to send His people into captivity in Babylon for 70 years. What was the real cause of their captivity? Religion at that time was at an all-time high. The people were not sent into captivity because they were not religious or because they were atheists. Jeremiah 23 has the answers as to why God's people were sent into captivity.

Jeremiah 23:1 states, "*Woe be unto the pastors that destroy and scatter the sheep of my pasture! saith the LORD.*" God placed a woe on these pastors and describes them in verses 13-15, "*And I have seen folly in the prophets of Samaria; they prophesied in Baal, and caused my people Israel to err. I have seen also in the prophets of Jerusalem an horrible thing: they commit adultery, and walk in lies: they strengthen also the hands of evildoers, that none* doth return from his wickedness: they are all of them unto me as Sodom, and the inhabitants thereof as Gomorrah. Therefore thus said the LORD of hosts concerning the prophets; Behold, I will feed them with wormwood, and make them drink the water of gall: for from the prophets of Jerusalem is profaneness...."

Jeremiah is describing these profane people who are spreading lies and encouraging evildoers, and who are under the woe of Almighty God. Verse 21 continues the description of these pastors, "I have not sent these prophets, yet they ran: I have no spoken to them, yet they prophesied."

Verse 26 says, "How long shall this be in the heart of the prophets that prophesy lies? yea, they are prophets of the deceit of their own heart."

Verses 31 and 32 state, "Behold, I am against the prophets, saith the LORD, that use their tongues, and say, He saith. Behold, I am against them that prophesy false dreams, saith the LORD, and do tell them, and cause my people to err by their lies, and by their lightness; yet I sent them not, nor commanded them: therefore they shall not prophet this people at all, saith the LORD."

Verse 34 continues, "And as for the prophet, and the priest, and the people, that shall say, The burden of the LORD, I will even punish that man and his house."

Verses 39 and 40 say, "Therefore, behold, I, even I, will utterly forget you, and I will forsake you, and the city that I gave you and your fathers, and cast you out of my presence: And I will bring an everlasting reproach upon you, and a perpetual shame, which shall not be forgotten."

God described these pastors upon whom He had sent a woe: (1) There was folly in them. (2) A horrible thing was seen in them. (3) They walked in lies. (4) They were like Sodom and Gomorrah. (5) They were profane. (6) God had not sent them and had not spoken unto them. (7) They were deceitful in their hearts. (8) Twice God said that He was against them. (9) These men caused the people to err by their lies. (10) They were light or shallow. God promised to punish these pastors and to utterly forget them, forsake them, and to forsake the city of Jerusalem. God also said that He would bring shame and reproach upon them. What a bunch of rascals those preachers must have been!

God sent captivity on the children of Israel because of the wickedness of these pastors. Many think that Israel was taken into captivity because they were whoremongers and liars and thieves and profane people. No! This was a nation at its religious zenith. These ungodly preachers caused God to send His people into captivity. These prophets caused the temple to be destroyed. They caused the walls around the city to be leveled. Their sinfulness brought a grievous famine to the land, which resulted in some mothers taking their own children and cooking them to feed the rest of their family. These prophets caused two generations of Israelites to grow up 500 miles from home under the rule of Nebuchadnezzar and the kingdoms that followed him.

What exactly did these prophets do that caused God to make such horrible statements about them?

1. These men substituted visions for the Word of God. Notice Jeremiah 23:16, "*Thus saith the LORD of hosts, Hearken not unto the words of the prophets that prophesy unto you: they make you vain: they speak a **vision** of their own heart, and not out of the mouth of the LORD.*" These wicked men spoke visions instead of the Word of God. Does this sound familiar? Do you know of anyone who said that he saw a vision of a 900-foot Jesus? Do you know anyone who had a vision that he would die if he didn't get a certain amount of money?

In verse 16, God warned His people not to listen to these prophets. The words *hearken not* mean "don't pay any attention to them." God said, "What My people need is the Word of God, not your visions."

Christians turn on the television and watch these false

teachers, the same kind who caused the destruction of Israel. That same crowd will someday stand guilty before God with the blood of America on their hands. Why? Because they are giving visions instead of the Word of God. The greatest enemy to America today is the charismatic movement.

One day I turned to the 700 Club on television. I heard one of the charismatics' key leaders say something like this, "I see a person with a suffering gall bladder." No, he didn't see a suffering gall bladder; he was preying upon the emotions of the people. He was trying to give the people some security because they believed he saw visions. He also said, "I see a back that hurts." Well, good night, just about everyone I know has back pain. He couldn't miss! No, he didn't see a vision; and neither did any of the other charismatic preachers.

2. These preachers substituted prophecy for the Word of God. Jeremiah 23:21 says, "*I have not sent these prophets, yet they ran: I have not spoken to them, yet they **prophesied**.*" As I continued to watch the 700 Club, the same leader said, "I have a word of prophesy." No, he didn't! I think that some charismatic people are patriotic, decent, and moral Americans. I agree with them that Christians should fight abortion and fight the freedom for the homosexuals' move-ment. However, as far as what the charismatics preach, you don't hear much Bible. Instead, you hear, "I have a word of prophecy." No, the charismatic don't have a word of prophe-cy. I have the Book of prophecy in my hands—the Bible!

Verse 22 says, "*But if they had stood in my counsel, and had caused my people to hear my words....*" What does God want His people to hear? His words! What this old country needs is the Bible, and instead of preachers saying, "I've seen an infect-ed gall bladder," they should be saying, "I've seen an infected sinner, and what he needs is the Word of God!"

Verse 22 continues, "*...then they should have turned them from their evil way, and from the evil of their doings.*" Organizing all the anti-homosexual campaigns and anti-abortion movements won't change anyone. The Word of God changes people. All the words of knowledge and visions will not clean up America. The Bible says in Psalm 119:30, "*The entrance of thy words giveth light,…*" and Psalm 119:9 says, "*Wherewithal shall a young man cleanse his way? by taking heed thereto according to thy word.*"

You ask, "Brother Hyles, don't you think some people can prophesy the future?" Sure I do. The Bible calls them soothsayers. God also tells His people to stay away from them, because they have satanic power.

3. These preachers substituted dreams for the Word of God. Jeremiah 23:25 says, "*I have heard what the prophets said, that prophesy lies in my name, saying, I have **dreamed**, I have dreamed.*" Makes you feel like you are watching a charismatic preacher on television, doesn't it?

Verses 27 and 28 state, "*Which think to cause my people to forget my name by their dreams which they tell every man to his neighbour, as their fathers have forgotten my name for Baal. The prophet that hath a dream, let him tell a dream; and he that hath my word, let him speak my word faithfully. What is the chaff to the wheat? saith the LORD.*" The dreams are called *chaff*, and God's Word is called *wheat*. Wheat feeds and nourishes people; chaff does not. Wheat is real; chaff is counterfeit.

On that same 700 Club program, a guest was introduced who said, "I'd like to speak about a dream that God gave me." God didn't give him that dream! Those onions he ate before he went to bed gave him that dream! God said, "My Word is better than your dream is. Give them My words."

Who are these liars and false teachers who are guilty of the destruction of the nation of Israel? Who are these pastors causing the nation of Israel to be taken into captivity? Who are these preachers who caused the destruction of the temple and the leveling of the walls and the great famine? Who are these prophets that caused the judgment of God upon Israel? They were pastors who preached visions and prophecies and dreams instead of preaching God's Word.

Verse 29 says, "*Is not my word like as a fire? saith the* LORD; *and like a hammer that breaketh the rock in pieces?*" What burns out the dross? The Word of God. Dreams? No! Visions? No! Prophecy? No! Only the Word of God. What is the hammer that breaks the rock into pieces? Dreams? No, Sir! Visions? No, Sir! Prophecies? No, Sir! This modern charismatic movement is very exciting because it preys on your emotions, but I would not give you one dime for every bit of emotion in this world that is not based on a Bible truth.

Someone sings a little ditty of a song like, "I've got a dog that got sick, but he got well, so I believe in God." That ditty has a peppy tune so the listeners shout, "Oh, glory, praise the LORD!" Not me, Brother! I shout about songs with words like these words:

> *Come, Thou Fount of ev'ry blessing,*
> *Tune my heart to sing Thy grace;*
> *Streams of mercy, never ceasing,*
> *Call for songs of loudest praise....*
>
> *O to grace how great a debtor.*
> *Daily I'm constrained to be!*
> *Let Thy goodness, like a fetter,*
> *Bind my wand'ring heart to Thee.*

That's what I shout about. I wouldn't give you a dime for all the emotion in the world that are not built on the Words of God.

God was saying that these people who live on their visions have nothing more than what **they** say is the Word of God. When they declare, "God gave me a vision. God spoke to me." God didn't do either one! That's a false version of the Bible!

Then there are those who say, "I have a word of prophecy." That is a false version of the Bible! Another says, "God spoke to me through a dream." That's a false version of the Bible!

God did not speak to man through a vision or a prophecy or a dream. No! God spoke to man through His Book. Every time a man says, "I have a word of prophecy" or "I had a vision" or "God spoke to me through a dream," he is stealing the Word of God from you. Jeremiah 23:30 says, "*Therefore, behold, I am against the prophets, saith the LORD, that steal my words every one from his neighbour.*"

Folks who live on visions have nothing more than an unprinted false bible. Folks who say that God has spoken to them through their dreams have nothing more than an unprinted false Bible. Those who talk about their words of prophecy have nothing more than an unprinted false Bible. They are doing the same thing that the translators of the NIV did; they are saying, "This is what God said." The truth is that God says it through His words.

4. These prophets substituted words of knowledge for God's Word. Jeremiah 23:31 and 32 say, "*Behold, I am against the prophets, saith the LORD, that use their tongues, and say, **He saith**. Behold, I am against them that prophesy false dreams, saith the LORD, and do tell them, and cause my people to err by their lies, and by their lightness; yet I sent them not, nor commanded them: therefore they shall not profit this people at all, saith the LORD.*"

On that same charismatic telecast, I saw men and women who were not married to each other holding hands around a circle, and each one of them were getting "words of knowledge." One lady said, "I have a word of knowledge from the Lord." No you don't, honey! God said that your word of knowledge is a false version of the Bible.

Nine times on that same telecast I heard men and women say, "I have a word of knowledge from the Lord." God said that He didn't send you, Mr. Charismatic Preacher. You did not see that 900-foot Jesus, and you didn't get that vision that you were going to die if you didn't get that $8 million. You used that to prey upon the minds of people to try to get their money! If you charismatic preachers can heal people, why do you build hospitals?

These prophets described in Jeremiah caused the destruction of Israel. They caused the 70-year captivity. These pastors caused the destruction of the temple and the destruction of the walls of their homes and the famine and the judgment of Almighty God. God called them liars and said they were like Sodom and Gomorrah. God said, "I am against you."

5. These prophets substituted tongues for the Word of God. Notice the word *tongues* in Jeremiah 23:31: "*Behold I am against the prophets, saith the LORD, that use their* **tongues,** *and say, He saith.*" On that same telecast, when one of those gals was praying, when all of a sudden she started jabbering some unintelligible garbage. God said, "Shut up! Get My Words!"

Don't ever think that someone else has something from God that you don't have because he is talking in some kind of a "tongue." God said that people who spoke in tongues were the cause of the destruction of Israel. They used their tongues and said, "God hath said."

The homosexuals will not cause the destruction of America. The baby killers will not cause the destruction of America. When God destroys this nation, He can write on America's tombstone as an epitaph, "Our preachers substituted visions and words of prophecy and dreams and words of knowledge and tongues for the words of Almighty God." They are all false versions of the Bible because they contain words that someone says that God said. God did not say them.

What will save America? What will save the dope traffic? The Word of God. What will save the liquor traffic? The words of Almighty God. We can clean up America with the Word of God.

You say, "Brother Hyles, doesn't God ever lead you?" Sure He does. He leads me by controlling my mind. Philippians 2:5 says, *"Let this mind be in you, which was also in Christ Jesus."* Yield your mind to Him and let God give you the sense to make the right decision.

6. These prophets substituted burdens for the Word of God. Jeremiah 23:33-35 says, *"And when this people, or the prophet, or a priest, shall ask thee, saying, What is the burden of the LORD? thou shalt then say unto them, What burden? I will even forsake you, saith the LORD. And as for the prophet, and the priest, and the people, that shall say, The **burden** of the LORD, I will even punish that man and his house. Thus shall ye say every one to his neighbour, and every one to his brother, What hath the LORD answered? And, What hath the LORD spoken?"* These prophets were saying, "The Lord has laid a burden on my heart." But God said, "Let's hear what I have to say."

You would be shocked at how many Baptist people are just as guilty as the NIV people are by saying, "God has spoken to me." No, He hasn't! He speaks to man through His Book. Some Christians say, "God has laid a burden on my heart." That is what the prophets said in Jeremiah's day.

Verses 36-38 say, *"And **the burden of the LORD shall ye mention no more**: for every man's word shall be his burden; for ye have perverted the words of the living God, of the LORD of hosts our God. Thus shalt thou say to the prophet, What hath the LORD answered thee? and, What hath the LORD spoken? But since ye say, The burden of the LORD; therefore thus saith the LORD; Because ye say this word, The burden of the LORD, and I have sent unto you, saying, **Ye shall not say, The burden of the LORD.**"*

Preachers will say, "This is the message that God has laid on my heart." That's not true. The message may be the one that God has led your mind to choose. I've preached over 56,000 sermons, and I'll be honest with you, God has never spoken to me about preaching a sermon. I have prayed hour upon hour every week and said, "God, I want my people to have what they need. Control my mind. Let Your mind be in my mind so I can choose the sermon they need to hear."

What am I supposed to preach? I am to preach something from the Book—the Word of God. We Baptist people have become guilty of having our own versions of the Bible.

Where should I preach? I am to preach somewhere in the world. Some preacher boys worry themselves to death over where God wants them to go to preach. They wait for some sign. One fellow told me that God wanted him to go to Minnesota because he read Ezekiel 48, and a portion of that Scripture talked about the north.

I asked, "What if you lived in Minnesota and read that? Would you go to the Arctic Circle?" A preacher boy will be much better off if he will say, "What should I preach?" Then he should ask God to control his mind as he chooses which of God's words to preach. Then he should ask God to control his mind as he chooses where to go in the world.

Sometimes God will miraculously direct and lead a man, but I'll guarantee you, He won't do it through visions or words of prophecy or dreams or words of knowledge or tongues or through the statement "God has given me a burden." He won't! Those are false bibles that have not been printed.

I know something about the power of the Word of God. The Bible is what people need. In the entire twenty-third chapter of Jeremiah, God is explaining to His people why He is going to send them into captivity and destroy their cities and their country. He will destroy it because of the pastors, religious leaders, prophets, and priests who say that God has spoken to them in visions and not by God's words. He will destroy it because of those who say that God has spoken to them in words of prophecy and not God's words. Those who say that God has spoken to them in dreams and not God's words have caused the captivity. Those who say that God has spoken to them in a word of knowledge and not God's words have caused the captivity. Those who say that God has spoken to them through tongues and not God's words have caused the captivity. Those who say that God has spoken to them through a burden and not God's words have caused the captivity of God's people.

The Bible is what people need and not all the unprinted false versions of the Bible.

Chapter Eleven
The King James Bible vs. the American Standard Version and the NASV

When I attended East Texas Baptist College of Marshall, Texas, (now East Texas Baptist University) and Southwestern Seminary, my professors said, "We use the King James Bible, but probably the most authentic and most dependable of all the Bibles is the American Standard Version." Today, most self-acclaimed scholars consider the *New American Standard Version* to be the best of the so-called other Bibles.

Let me make it very plain. The *American Standard Version*, like all the other false Bibles, does not come from the same manuscripts as the King James Bible. This subject has been discussed in chapter one. In review, the King James Bible comes from the *Textus Receptus*, and the other versions come from the manuscripts compiled by Westcott and Hort, professors at Cambridge University. The following quotes are from Mr. Hort's autobiography:

- "Evangelicals seem to be perverted rather than untrue."

- "The book that has most engaged me is Darwin [the famous evolutionist]. My feeling is strong that the theory is unanswerable."

- "I have been persuaded for many years that Mary-worship and Jesus-worship have very much in common."

- "I am inclined to believe that such a state as Eden never existed."

- "The popular doctrine of substitution [the vicarious death that Christ died for us] is an immoral and a material counterfeit."

- "The Romish view seems to me nearer and more likely to lead to the truth than the evangelical. We dare not forsake the sacraments, or God will forsake us."

There's more to the King James Bible issue than a bunch of independent Baptist fundamentalists trying to cause a ruckus. Folks just pick up a version of the Bible and assume that someone wanted to make the Bible easier for them to understand.

Let's hear from Mr. Westcott, "No one now, I suppose, holds that the first three chapters of Genesis give a literal history."

These quotations are just specimen statements from these men who have given the world the Catholic manuscripts that were kept in the Vatican in Rome.

The *American Standard Version* and the *New American Standard Version* change or omit over 5,000 passages of Scripture from the King James Bible. Let's compare some of the differences in the King James Bible and the *American Standard Version*. In so doing, I will show you how Westcott and Hort were attacking the fundamentals of the faith.

In the King James Bible, John 3:36 says, *"He that believeth on the Son hath everlasting life: and he that believeth not the Son shall not see life; but the wrath of God abideth on him."* The

NASV says, "He who does not obey the son." That wording is nothing more than salvation by works. With changes like that, I am not surprised when Mr. Hort said that it is heresy to believe in the substitutionary death of Christ. The next time you pick up the NASV, don't just think it is some Bible that theologians have published to make the Bible easier to understand. It is an attack of the Devil at the foundation of the faith of our Lord Jesus Christ. **First, the doctrine of salvation is attacked by the ASV and the NASV.**

In the King James Bible, John 6:35 says, *"And Jesus said unto them, I am the bread of life: he that cometh to me shall never hunger.... "* This verse is talking about the security of the believer. If you come to Christ, you will never hunger again. The NASV says, "He that cometh to me shall not hunger." What difference does that make? It makes a lot of difference. For example, saying, "I am not hungry; I just ate," is not the same as "I never will be hungry." Jesus said that if a person comes to Him, he will never get hungry again. He is saved forever! Not only has the doctrine of salvation been attacked, but likewise, **the doctrine of the sustaining, persevering power of the Gospel of Jesus Christ has been attacked.** Brother, when you got saved, you got saved for keeps, forever! The Bible teaches again and again that salvation is eternal, and that there is eternal security of the believer in Christ Jesus. The person who comes to Jesus will never hunger again.

In the King James Bible, John 6:47 says, *"Verily, verily, I say unto you, He that believeth on me hath everlasting life."* The NASV leaves out the words *on me*. **Salvation in Christ is being attacked.** He that believeth what? He that believeth the sun rises in the east and sets in the west? He that believeth that the Cubs will never win a pennant? He that believeth what? It is not believing that saves a person. It is believing on Christ that saves a person. The NASV not only changes the words of God; it changes and omits the words of Jesus that He spoke on earth. Not only is the NASV calling God's words a liar, it is also calling the Son of God a liar. Jesus said, "If you believe on me," and the NASV said, "If you believe." I'm not going to mess with a Bible that attacks salvation, the security of the believer, and the Person of salvation.

In the King James Bible, Luke 2:33 says, *"And Joseph and his mother marvelled at those things which were spoken of him."* Why doesn't this verse say, "his father and his mother?" Because in this verse, the Bible is teaching the virgin birth. Joseph was not Jesus' father, and the Holy Spirit was very careful in this reference to say, "Joseph and his mother." Mary was the mother of Jesus' earthly body, but Joseph was not the father of His earthly body. The seed that was planted in the womb of Mary was placed there by the Holy Spirit. The NASV says, "his father and mother." **The virgin birth of our Saviour is being attacked.** Joseph was not Jesus' father because Mary had not known a man. It wasn't the fact that she didn't have a husband; it was the fact that she did not have *any* man. God placed the seed in Mary by His Holy Spirit, and when Jesus was born, Mary was still a virgin. Joseph was not the father of Jesus.

In the King James Bible, Luke 4:3 and 4 say, *"And the devil said unto him, If thou be the Son of God, command this stone that it be made bread. And Jesus answered him, saying, It is written, That man shall not live by bread alone, but by every word of God."* Since these NASV people do not believe that every word of God has been preserved, don't be surprised that the NASV leaves out the phrase, "but by every word of God." If I did not believe that the Bible has been preserved for this generation, I would want to leave out that part of the verse, too! Again, not only are the translators attacking the printed Word of God, they are also attacking the words that Jesus used. The ASV and NASV are taking an ax and chopping at the foundation and the fundamentals of the faith of our fathers. They are chopping at salvation, the security of the believer, the Person of Christ for salvation, the virgin birth of Christ, and now **they are attacking the Word of God.**

In the King James Bible, Colossians 1:14 says, *"In whom we have redemption through his blood, even the forgiveness of sins."* The NASV leaves out, "through his blood." Jesus could not forgive one single sin if it were not for the shedding of the blood. On the Passover night when the Lord came through the land, He could not have allowed anyone to live without the blood on the door posts. That decision was not based on the sincerity of the father of the house nor on the religious activities going on in the house or the church affiliation of the people in the house nor on how the people lived inside the house. The question was, "Was the blood on the door posts?"

On the Day of Atonement, when the high priest went inside the Holy of Holies to sprinkle the blood of the innocent substitute on the mercy seat of the ark of the covenant, it was not how good those people were; it was whether or not the blood was on the mercy seat. Jesus could not forgive because He died; He forgave because He shed His blood. We're not just talking about the *Reader's Digest Version* or the *Living Bible.* This heresy is creeping into our nondenominational and Baptist schools. I'm talking about theologians promoting themselves as Bible scholars but who don't even believe the Bible. They are teaching in our colleges and universities, and I'm not just talking about Rochester Seminary or Southern Methodist University or Baylor University or Fuller Seminary. I'm referring to schools that put on their sign that they believe the Bible, but then they teach from the *American Standard Version* and the *New American Standard Version.* **These theologians are taking away the blood.** They are taking away salvation. They are taking away the vicarious death. They are taking away the virgin birth. They are taking away the security of the believer, but they are not going to do it without my taking all the strength I have to tell the world what those rascals are doing.

II Timothy 3:15-17, *"And that from a child thou hast known the holy scriptures, which are able to make thee wise unto salvation through faith which is in Christ Jesus. All scripture is given by inspiration of God, and is profitable for doctrine, for reproof, for correction, for instruction in righteousness: That the man of God may be perfect, throughly furnished unto all good works."* What is able to make a person wise unto salvation? The Holy Scriptures. That means nobody can get saved without the Holy Scriptures. Peter says a person is not born of corruptible seed. The ASV reads, "Every scripture inspired by God is profitable for doctrine." The King James Bible says, *"All scripture."* In other words, the ASV translators are saying that there are some Scriptures that are not inspired by God.

Let's review the verbal plenary inspiration of the Scriptures. The word *verbal* means that every word of the Bible is inspired. *Plenary* means that the entire Bible is inspired word for word. Verbal inspiration says, "Look at a word in the Bible; it is inspired of God." Plenary inspiration says, "Every word in the Bible is inspired by God; all of it is inspired by God." The Westcott and Hort people say, "Every scripture that is inspired by God." These translators are saying that all Scripture is not inspired by God. Every Scripture is inspired by God! **The inspiration of the Scripture is being attacked.**

In the King James Bible, I Peter 4:1 and 2 say, *"Forasmuch then as Christ has suffered for us in the flesh, arm yourselves likewise with the same mind: for he that hath suffered in the flesh hath ceased from sin; That he no longer should live the rest of his time in the flesh to the lusts of men, but to the will of God."* The ASV leaves out the words *for us*, which is why Jesus suffered in the flesh. He suffered for us! **These translators are attacking the vicarious death.**

In the King James Bible, Genesis 6:8 says, *"But Noah found grace in the eyes of the* L ORD*."* The NASV says, "And Noah found favor in the eyes of the Lord." What is the difference between favor and grace? There are two kinds of favor: merited and unmerited. Grace is unmerited favor. If I favor Brother Colsten over Brother Young because Brother Colsten is nicer than Brother Young, I'm favoring Brother Colsten. But if I favor Brother Colsten for no reason at all, that's grace. When these translators say, "Noah found favor in the eyes of the Lord," they are saying that God looked down and was proud of Noah, so Noah found favor with God because of what he had done. Grace is not favor because of what Noah had done. Grace is favor because of what God had done. Yes, grace is favor, but it is more than favor. It is only the kind of favor that is not deserved.

Not one person deserves to get saved, but God saved you; that's grace. You deserve to go to Hell, but you're not going to Hell; that is grace. You're going to Heaven even though you don't deserve to go to Heaven; that's grace. You're a child of God, but you don't deserve to be a child of God; that's grace. The word *favor* in this verse is very much in keeping with the works salvation of Mr. Westcott and Mr. Hort. They are saying that the reason Noah was spared was because of the good works of Noah; however, Noah wasn't saved because of what he did; He was saved because of what God did! **Westcott and Hort have changed the Bible to take away even the grace of Almighty God.**

These translators changed the Bible to take away the plan of salvation. They changed it to take away the security of the believer. They changed God's words to take away the Person of salvation. They changed it to take away the virgin birth of Christ. They changed it to take away the blood of Christ. They changed it to take away the vicarious death of Christ. They changed it to take away the fact that man lives by every word of God. They have changed it to take away the grace of God.

Let me show how these "bibles" attack and cast reflection and doubt on the deity of Jesus Christ.

In the King James Bible, I Timothy 3:16 says, *"And without controversy great is the mystery of godliness: God was manifest in the flesh, justified in the Spirit, seen of angels, preached unto the Gentiles, believed on in the world, received up into glory."*

Notice the line, *"God was manifest in the flesh."* In the King James Bible, the word is *"manifest."* The *New American Standard Version* changes "manifest" to "revealed"; "God was revealed in the flesh." The word *revealed* means, "to show something." The word *manifest* is a stronger word that means "to prove by showing plainly."

I am revealed in the flesh. Each of us is revealed in the flesh, but we are not manifested in the flesh. The NASV lowers Jesus to the level of man by saying, "God was revealed in the flesh," instead of "God was manifest in the flesh."

In the King James Bible, Romans 14:10 says, *"But why dost thou judge thy brother? or why dost thou set at nought thy brother? for we shall all stand before the judgment seat of Christ."* The *American Standard Version* changes the word *Christ* to "God." It says, "We must all stand before the judgment seat of God."

That change takes away the deity of Christ. When a person stands before the judgment seat of Christ, he is standing before the judgment seat of God. Christ is God. He is just as much God as God the Father is God. He is just as much God as God the Holy Spirit is God. Jesus is God. Replacing "the judgment seat of Christ" with "the judgment seat of God," is saying that Jesus is not God. When you insert the word *Christ* you are writing the word **God** as much as you write the word **Christ** because "C-H-R-I-S-T" spells "God."

In the King James Bible, Acts 20:28 says, *"Take heed therefore unto yourselves, and to all the flock, over the which the Holy Ghost hath made you overseers, to feed the church of God, which he hath purchased with his own blood."*

Notice the words, *"which he hath purchased with his own blood."* The word *"he"* is referring to God the Father. The NASV says, "obtained with the blood of his son."

Any doctor will tell you that when a child is born, the blood is supplied by the father. The blood is determined by the father. Jesus' blood was not the same kind of blood that you and I have. If Joseph had been Jesus' father, Jesus would have had blood that was sinful blood. Jesus did not have the blood of a man; he had the blood of God. The seed of the Holy Spirit was placed in the womb of Mary, which means that God, the Holy Spirit, was the One Who implanted the seed in Mary that brought forth the Lord Jesus Christ. God's blood was in Jesus. The blood of Jesus is actually God's blood. When Jesus shed His own blood, He was actually shedding the blood of the Father. The NASV says, "No, it was Jesus' blood." Once again, the NASV is trying to bring down the Lord Jesus Christ from being God to being simply a man. That is why it was necessary for the virgin birth. If Jesus was born of a virgin, then God supplied the blood.

The question comes, "Could Jesus have sinned?" No, Jesus could not have sinned. Every once in a while somebody says, "Well, Jesus could have sinned just like we could." No, He could not. He could have been tempted as much as we are tempted. The Bible says that Jesus was in all points tempted like we are. Likewise, it was just as hard for Him not to sin as it was for us, but He could not have sinned. Why? Because according to Leviticus 17:11, the life of the flesh is in the blood, and God, the Holy Spirit provided Jesus' blood. Since the blood came from God through the Father's bloodline, then Jesus had sinless blood; therefore, Jesus could not have sinned because He did not have sinful blood in Him. He could have been tempted because He was the son of Mary; however, He could not sin because he was Son of God. He could have been tested and tempted to do wrong because He was the Son of

Mary, but He could not do wrong because He was the Son of God.

In the King James Bible, John 9:35 says, *"Jesus heard that they had cast him out; and when he had found him, he said unto him, Dost thou believe on the Son of God?"*

That question in the NASV says, "Dost thou believe on the son of man?" This change is just another in a series of efforts to bring down the deity of Christ to the level of man.

In the King James Bible, Matthew 1:25 says, *"And knew her not till she had brought forth her firstborn son: and he called his name JESUS."* The NASV omits the word "firstborn" and reads, "And knew her not till she had brought forth her son." This omission questions the virgin birth. Even if Jesus was born without an earthly father, and if he was not Mary's first-born son, this omission implies that she could have had a previous son; therefore, she would not have been a virgin. Take away the "firstborn," and you've got just another son.

The simple truth is, Mary had never known a man when Jesus Christ was born. Some say, "What difference does it make if Jesus was born without Mary knowing a man?" It makes a tremendous difference because it makes Isaiah 7:14 untrue when it says, *"…Behold, a virgin shall conceive…."*

Think about the word, *worship*. Matthew 4:10 says that we are to worship only God. That means when Jesus accepted worship from others, He was admitting that He was God. Matthew 4:10 says we're to worship only God; so if Jesus had not been God, then He would not have allowed people to worship Him. The fact that He accepted worship means that He was admitting the fact that He was the very God of gods—as much God as God the Father, and as much God as the Holy Spirit.

In Revelation, an angel came to John on the Isle of Patmos to reveal the events of the end times. In Revelation 22:8 and 9, the Bible says that John fell down to worship the angel and the angel said, "Worship God; don't worship me."

Acts 10:25 and 26 contains the story of Peter going soul winning to the house of Cornelius as the Holy Spirit had directed him. When Peter arrived, Cornelius had been studying the Word of God. The Bible says that Cornelius fell down before Peter, and Peter said, "...Stand up; I myself also am a man." All of these verses teach that we are to worship only God. The fact that Jesus allowed and encouraged people to worship Him proves that He was God.

In the King James Bible, Matthew 9:18 states, "While he spake these things unto them, behold, there came a certain ruler, and worshipped him, saying, My daughter is even now dead: but come and lay thy hand upon her, and she shall live." When this certain ruler came to Jesus and worshipped Him, Jesus didn't say, "Don't worship me. I am only a man." The very fact that Jesus allowed this ruler to worship Him means that Jesus was saying, "I am God." The American Standard Version replaces the words, "worshipped him," with "bowed down before him." So in the ASV, Matthew 9:18 says, "While he spake these things unto them, behold, there came a certain ruler, and bowed down before him."

Wait a minute! You can bow down before anybody. By replacing the word, "worship" with "bowed down," the ASV is saying that Jesus is not God, and that makes me want to have some teeth prints in my knuckles. Jesus is God!—the very God!—and is deserving of worship!

In the King James Bible, Matthew 20:20 says, "Then came to him the mother of Zebedee's children with her sons, worshipping him, and desiring a certain thing of him." Did Jesus rebuke this woman and her children for worshipping Him? No! Jesus was saying that He was, in fact, God.

The New American Standard Version changes the word, "worshipping," to "bowing down." The verse says, "Then came to him the mother of Zebedee's children with her sons, bowing down before him." In the King James Bible, Mark 5:6 says, *"But when he saw Jesus afar off, he ran and worshipped him."* The NASV says, "he ran and bowed down before him."

In the King James Bible, Luke 24:52 says, *"And they worshipped him, and returned to Jerusalem with great joy."* The NASV says, "they bowed down before him."

We need a generation of people who love the Bible and who believe in the deity of Jesus Christ. Anything that even casts the slightest shadow on the deity of Christ bothers me greatly. Let's underline the deity of Christ and not put it in small letters. Don't put a shadow on it. Don't put it in the fog. Let's put it in bold print, capital letters, and underline it. **JESUS IS THE VERY GOD OF GODS!**

Folks bow down to the Pope. Folks bow down to the Queen of England. Don't you see that the *New American Standard Version* is lowering Jesus to the same level as the Pope and the Queen of England?

In Acts 8:36-38, we read the story of Philip and the eunuch. *"And as they went on their way, they came unto a certain water: and the eunuch said, See, here is water; what doth hinder me to be baptized? And Philip said, If thou believest with all thine heart, thou mayest. And he answered and said, I believe that Jesus Christ is the Son of God."* Notice the statement, *"I believe that Jesus Christ is the Son of God."* That statement means that Jesus was virgin born. *"And he commanded the chariot to stand still: and they went down both into the water, both Philip and the eunuch; and he baptized him."*

In the *New American Standard Version*, those three verses are in brackets. Written beside those three verses is, "Probably not in the originals."

In the first place, self-styled scholars, when did you see the originals? Nobody for several thousands of years has seen a copy of any of the originals. "Probably not in the originals" is simply the kind of language that scholars like to use to make lay people think they are smart. Tell me, who has ever seen the originals? No professor at any Bible institute has ever seen the originals. No professor at any seminary has ever seen the originals. No professor at any nondenominational university has ever seen the originals. By the way, I've got as much right to make the statement, "It's not in the originals" as they do. I could choose any verse in the Bible that I don't want in there and say, "Probably not in the originals." The truth is, those theologians haven't got the foggiest idea whether or not it is in the originals. There's nothing near the originals available for anybody. That statement makes a person wonder if these theologians want to leave out, "I believe that Jesus is the Son of God."

The following are other references in which the *American Standard Version* and the *New American Standard Version* have changed or omitted words or phrases:

Matthew 23:14	Luke 7:31	John 5:3, 4
Mark 7:16	Luke 9:54	John 6:47
Mark 9:24	Luke 11:29	John 7:53-8:11
Mark 9:42	Luke 17:36	John 8:16
Mark 10:21	Luke 22:31	John 11:41
Mark 11:10	Luke 23:17	John 16:16
Mark 11:26	Luke 23:19, 20	John 17:12
Mark 12:29, 30	Luke 23:43	Acts 2:30
Mark 13:14	Luke 24:12	Acts 7:30
Mark 15:28	Luke 24:40	Acts 7:37
Mark 16:9, 10	Luke 24:49	Acts 8:37
Luke 1:28	Luke 24:51	Acts 9:5-6
Luke 2:33	John 1:14	Acts 10:6
Luke 2:43	John 1:18	Acts 16:31
Luke 4:4	John 3:13	Acts 17:26
Luke 4:8	John 3:15	Romans 1:16
Luke 4:41	John 4:42	Romans 5:2

Romans 9:28	I Corinthians 5:7	II Corinthians 4:6
Romans 11:6	I Corinthians 6:20	II Corinthians 4:10
Romans 13:9	I Corinthians 7:39	Galatians 3:1
Romans 14:6	I Corinthians 10:28	Galatians 4:7
Romans 14:9	I Corinthians 11:24	Galatians 6:15
Romans 14:21	I Corinthians 15:47	Ephesians 3:9
Romans 15:29	I Corinthians 11:29	
Romans 16:24	I Corinthians 16:22, 23	

These are just a few of the verses in the King James Bible that are changed or omitted in the *American Standard Version* and the *New American Standard*.

The entire wave of so-called Bibles is, on the surface, a money-making deal for publishers and others; but way back behind that motive, the Devil is trying to shake the foundations of the truth and the fundamentals of the old-time religion and the old-time Gospel.

Chapter Twelve

There Are Too Many Smiths in the Land

I Samuel 13:19 says, "*Now there was no smith found throughout all the land of Israel: for the Philistines said, Lest the Hebrews make them swords or spears.*" In those days, a smith was more of a manufacturer of weapons. He made swords and spears and weapons of war, but he also made farming equipment, such as hoes and sickles.

At the time of this text, there was only one sword, or at the most, two. Saul had a sword though at the time, Saul was not planning to use it, because Saul had been disenfranchised by God. Actually there was only one available sword for battle. This sword belonged to Jonathan, Saul's son. The Israelites were in a war with the Philistines, and the Israelites fought with only clubs and farming instruments. They even went to the enemy to get those sharpened. Near the border, smiths would set up shop and the farmers of Israel would go across the border to have the Philistine smiths sharpen their hoes and other farm machinery. Now they were in a war.

I Samuel 14:6 says, "*And Jonathan said to the young man that bare his armour, Come, and let us go over unto the garrison of these uncircumcised: it may be that the LORD will work for us....*" Bear in mind, here is one man with one sword and his armor bearer trying to fight the whole Philistine nation. Jonathan continued, "…*it may be the* LORD *will work for us: for there is no restraint to the* LORD *to save by many or by few.*" When Jonathan and his armor bearer climbed up in the rocks and started killing Philistines, something amazing happened. The Philistine army became so confused, they started killing each other. Saul and Jonathan watched the Philistines killing each other, thereby giving Israel the victory. The victory was won by Israel with just one sword.

I Samuel 14:22 says, "*Likewise all the men of Israel which had hid themselves in mount Ephraim, when they heard that the Philistines fled, even they also followed hard after them in the battle.*" The Israelite people were waiting to see who won (just like some of you!) After they saw what that one sword had done, they all joined and said, "We want to be on the winning side." They won the battle because they had no smiths in the land. God gave the victory to them to show that He was God and to show that God does it. If there had been enough Israelite smiths in the land to build a great arsenal of weapons, then credit for the victory would not have gone to God. But in this case, with no smiths in the land and only one sword owned by Jonathan, God gave the victory. So, the victory was given because there were no smiths in the land.

Today, we are also in a battle; we also have a Sword—the King James Bible, which is the only one we need. We have too many smiths in the land with too many people making new swords. God is the One Who gets the glory for the victory if we just use the one Sword that we have. We are in a battle, and the battle is the Lord's. Ephesians 6:17 tells us that the Sword is the Word of God. Hebrews 4:12 says, "*For the word of God is quick, and powerful, and sharper than any twoedged sword….*" We have a Sword, and we only need that one Sword. With just that one Sword, God's people will come nearer to winning the battle just like Jonathan did.

There can only be one Sword—only one Bible. Matthew

4:4 says, "...*Man shall not live by bread alone, but by every word that proceedeth out of the mouth of God.*" If man lives by every word of God, then there has to be a Book which contains every word of God.

Once I received a book from a publisher asking for my endorsement. The book was entitled, *Twenty-six Translations of the Bible.* That's 25 translations too many! Twenty-five of those 26 translations of the Bible do not contain every word of God. They differ in their translation concerning some of the words. If man lives by every word that proceedeth out of the mouth of God, we've got to have an every-word Bible.

John 15:7 says, "*If ye abide in me, and my words abide in you, ye shall ask what ye will, and it shall be done unto you.*" John 15:7 didn't say, "If my thoughts abide in you," or "If my message from Heaven abides in you." According to that verse, if we get our prayers answered, we have to have an every-word Bible.

By the Word of God we are saved. By the Word of God we are cleansed. The Word of God leads us. To know the will of God, we must have the words of God. We must have a pure Bible that contains the words of God.

John 14:23 says, "*Jesus answered and said unto him, If a man love me, he will keep my words....*" If we don't have His words, how can we keep them? Jesus didn't say to keep His paragraphs or translations or thoughts or message. Jesus said, "*...he will keep my words.*"

Both Mark 13:31 and Luke 21:33 say, "*Heaven and earth shall pass away: but my words shall not pass away.*" These two verses mean that there is some place in the world where God's words are. They have to be.

In our generation, there is nothing under attack more than the King James Bible. Nothing! You have one crowd that says, "We do not have the Word of God." Another crowd says, "We don't have the **words** of God, but the Bible has the **thoughts** of God." Still another crowd says, "The Bible was only inspired in the original." The average layman believes that somewhere in the world the originals exist. What a tragedy! When a church says in their articles of faith, "We believe that the Word of God was inspired in the original language," then the average person in that church thinks that maybe the originals have been found in the Dead Sea Scrolls. This belief is not true. There is no original in the world today, and nobody says they have one. No liberal preacher will say, "We have the original." If the only place in the world where we have a word-for-word inspired Bible is in the originals, that means that today there is no book that contains the words of God. That means we cannot get our prayers answered as written in John 15:7. That means that we cannot feed on the Word of God as mentioned in Matthew 4:4.

When I went to college, I believed I had the words of God in the King James Bible. I was in college for a while and then found out that not only didn't I have them, I couldn't have them! Not only that, I found out that nobody did. Not only that, I found out that there was no such thing as any book in the world that had the words of God in them. At least, that is what my professors taught me.

Here's what is happening in America. The old-time preachers who built this country believed that the King James Bible contained the words of God. Your grandparents who helped built this country shed their tears on the King James Bible, believing they had the very words of God in their hands. All fundamentalists believed that the King James Bible contained the words of God until we started our own colleges and seminaries and sent our professors to train at the feet of Karl Barth and Reinhold Niebuhr and others who said that the Bible does not have the "words" of God but is the "Word" of God. These men also said that all of the Bible is not inspired word for word. Some fundamentalists did not want to be considered uneducated by the highbrow, intellectual community.

They were not willing to be called nuts and fools. Just chalk me up as a nut! Chalk me up as a fool! Chalk me up as an uneducated illiterate if you want to, but I guarantee you I'd rather study my ABC's in Heaven than study Greek and Hebrew in Hell! Luke 9:26 says, *"For whosoever shall be ashamed of me and of my words, of him shall the Son of man be ashamed, when he shall come in his own glory, and in his Father's, and of the holy angels."* Theologians have ruined this country. It is very popular to say, "In the original, it says...." There is no original to look at. Or the theologian will say, "Within the *Amplified Bible*...." Do you know what that means? *Amplified* means "to blow something bigger, to make it more plain." Are you trying to tell me that they have made a new Bible that is more plain than the King James Bible? We built some pretty good old-fashioned churches on the King James Bible back when we had no smiths in the land.

Psalm 12:6 and 7 say, *"The words of the LORD are pure words: as silver tried in a furnace of earth, purified seven times. Thou shalt keep them, O LORD, thou shalt preserve them from this generation for ever."* Notice God said, *"words"*—not word.

I believe that every word in the King James Bible is the Word of God and I believe it always was. I believe the Word of God was already finished before the world was ever created. There never was a time when there were not the words of God. God dictated His words to holy men of old. Some will say, "But Paul wrote in his own style." No! The style was already written in Heaven, and God made Paul to match the words, not the words to match Paul. You may say, "I just don't believe that." You did before you went to seminary. There's not a preacher boy in America that didn't believe he had the words of God in his hands when he went to college. There he sat at the feet of some non-soul-winning, non-fiery, non-evangelistic, critical theologians who told him that we didn't have a Bible. I'm not referring to Harvard Divinity School. I'm referring to some of the fundamental schools where good people send their young people. I'm talking about schools and professors who disguise themselves as fundamentalists, who do not believe that there is a book in the world that contains the very words of God. We have too many smiths in the land.

The attack is on the Bible. I heard a man on a "Christian" radio station make this statement: "I cannot say that the King James Bible has the words of God, but I can say it has the message of God." My Bible does not say, "Man shall not live by bread alone but by every **message** that proceedeth out of the mouth of God." My Bible says, "*every word.*" I'm not going to keep my mouth shut any longer about people who are making light of the words of the Blessed Book. We need these words! I must have a Bible that has the words of God. We have too many smiths in the land.

The *New King James*, the *Revised Standard Version*, the *American Standard Version*, the *New Testament in Basic English*, the *Berkeley Version*, the *Moffatt Version*, the *New Testament in the Language of Today*, *Goodspeed*, *Amplified*, *Centenary Translation*, *Philip's New Testament in Modern English*, the *Emphasized New Testament*, the *Williams' Translation*, *Language of the People*, *Living Letters*, the *Living Bible*, the *New Scofield* not to mention all the others who have dared to meddle with the Word of God are all second-rate swords published by smiths who ought to be out soul winning instead of making new swords!

We need only one Sword. The smiths would have ruined the chance of the Israelites winning the war against the Philistines. God said, "I want to show you what I can do. Jonathan, just take your sword and go to battle." Jonathan took that one sword and won the war. If they had many smiths in the land and an arsenal of weapons so that all of the Israelites could have fought, then God would not have done it. God wanted to win a war with one sword. That's the way

God is going to win the battle in America today—with one Sword.

Somewhere there have to be the words of God; therefore, there must be just one Bible. If you don't believe it is the King James, pick one out; but there must be just one because the Bible teaches that we must have the words of God. When you start chopping up the Bible, then the next step is that the charismatics get on the television and say, "I had a revelation from God, just like the Bible is a revelation from God. Mine exceeds the Bible because I've gotten mine since the Bible was written." We've gone wild trying to let man give man a Bible.

In the book, *Twenty-Six Translations of the Bible*, the editor says, "For if thou open thy eyes and consider well the gift of the Holy Ghost therein, thou shalt see that one translation declareth, openeth, and illustrateth another, and that in many cases, one is plain commentary unto another."

He is saying that the translations need help. My Bible says that the Word of God is pure. He continues, "But for all the merits of the King James Version, the modern Bible reader finds it increasingly difficult to understand its archaic style and diction."

What he is saying is that those who choose the King James Bible are idiots and need some idiot language.

He says, "The aim of the present volume is to clarify the meaning of the King James Version by the use of more recent translations of the biblical text."

Let's compare some verses in the King James Bible with other so-called Bibles. In the *King James Bible*, Genesis 1:2 says, "*And the earth was without form, and void....*" The ASV says, "And the earth was waste and void...." Those words aren't the same, are they? We have to have a Bible that has every word, don't we? *The New American Bible* says, "a formless wasteland." *Young's Literal Translation* says, "had existed waste and void." *The Living Bible* says, "a shapeless, chaotic mass." Somebody is wrong! We have to have every word of God!

In the King James Bible, Isaiah 7:14 says, "...*Behold, a **virgin** shall conceive, and bear a son, and shall call his name Immanuel.*" One of the other versions says, "Behold, a **young woman** shall conceive." Can you see what is being done? They are attacking the virgin birth. Another says, "A **young woman** is with child." Another says, "See, a **maiden** shall conceive." Another says, "It is this, a **maiden** is with child and shall soon give birth." These are people who are getting paid to fiddle with the Bible.

John 3:16 says, "*For God so loved the world, that he gave his only begotten Son....*" The *Williams Version* says, "his only son." See the Devil's trick in taking out the word "**begotten**"? In the first place, Jesus is not the only son of God. I am a son of God too. Another version says, "the son, the only son." Another says, "his only begotten **unique** son." These verses not only take away from the Bible, they also add to it.

We used to say, "I just ain't got no more sense than to believe that this Book is the Word of God!" or "I'm just ignorant enough to believe every word in this old Book." We ought to say it again. In the first place, we ought to admit that we are ignorant. Even folks who are educated ought to admit they are ignorant. The only difference in educated folks and uneducated folks is that they are ignorant on different subjects.

In the second place, we ought to still believe that the Bible is the Word of God. Several years ago, a pulpit committee contacted me asking me to help them find a preacher for their church. They said there are two qualifications: He must never have been to the Holy Land, and he must never have taken Greek. I realized they were serious. I asked, "Why?" They said, "The whole church is sick and tired of seeing slides and hearing, 'in the original it says.'" Somebody wants to hear a preacher stand up and say, "I've got a Book from God, and I want to tell you what God has to say in His Book."

Where are the words of God? I hold in my hand the words of God—the King James Bible. I came to the place that I had to admit that we need the words of God, not just the thoughts of God. I had to admit it—The Bible says too much about it. I came to the place that I believed that somewhere in the world there were the words of God.

When I was in the U.S. Army, I was issued a rifle. In those days, mine was an M-1. The first thing I had to do was to learn to dismantle my rifle. I had to break down every piece, and then put every piece back together. Christians ought to study the Word of God in the same way. I can defend the Bible all I want, but if I don't read it, it doesn't do any good. I can say, "We have the words of God," but as long as the Bible stays closed on the coffee table, it doesn't do a bit of good. When the Lord said, "*Study to shew thyself approved unto God...*," He wasn't saying, "Read half a verse, a poem, and what Dr. So-and-So said." The Lord meant for every Christian to live in the Book.

Not only did I have to disassemble and reassemble by rifle, I had to keep it spotless and clean. Every Saturday, our sergeant came to the barracks for a white-glove inspection. He would run a rod with a white cloth on the end of it down into the barrel of our rifles. One Saturday, he found grease in my rifle. For one entire week, that sergeant made me tuck my rifle in bed at night, kiss it good night, tell it that I loved it, and I had to sleep on the floor beside my bed.

Not only do we need to believe the Bible, we need to treasure it, defend it, and read it. It is our foundation. Suppose the Lord came back tonight and say, "Did you believe My words?" Would you have to say, "Which ones?" You can't believe them all. If you believe them all and don't have a Bible with the very words of God, then you have to believe in thought inspiration or that the message is what is important and not the words. It comes back to the fact that we don't believe that we have an every-word Bible. What we have done is cater to whatever new fad comes out and give them a Bible to please them.

I'll guarantee you that the most avid Bible readers and the greatest Bible lovers today are still the people who stick with the King James Bible. The people who use the King James Bible are still the ones who best know the Bible. Do you think that you are going to make the hippies read the Bible because you change the words? If you change the words, you no longer have a Bible.

Let's be people of the Book. Let's defend it. Let's stand for it. Let's believe every word of it. Let me share one last thought. In the beginning of this chapter, I mentioned that the Israelites had only one sword. God's people took their substitute weapons, their hoes and farming equipment, to the enemy to get them sharpened. That's exactly what is happening now. We are denying the one Sword that God has given us, and we are taking our hoes to the enemy to be sharpened—but there is just one Sword. We're sharpening a bunch of plows—but there is just one Sword. We're sharpening a bunch of sickles—but there is just one Sword! I don't care how much you sharpen those hoes, they will not win a war. I've often thought about that crowd of Jews coming for the battle. One man carried his hoe; another had his plow to throw at the enemy. Jonathan comes with the only sword in the land and wins the battle.

America needs to get back to the King James Bible. The Bible would solve all the congressional hearings. It would solve all the problems with the pacifists. The words of God would solve the economic problems in this country. It would solve the agricultural problems. It would solve the educational problems. But too many don't believe it. When I face the Lord, I'd rather tell Him I believed it too much than too little.

We have too many smiths in the land making second-rate weapons for the battle of God. Let's fire all the smiths! We just need one Sword—the King James Bible!

Chapter Thirteen

Keep Your Stinking Feet Out of My Drinking Water

Years ago, a lady visited our church on a Sunday morning. She came back again Sunday night. After the service, she asked one of our members, "Which one of those preachers is the pastor of this church—the guy who was loving and sweet on Sunday morning or the guy who was mean on Sunday night?"

Billy Sunday used to say, "You can't love flowers unless you hate weeds." You can't love health unless you hate germs. You can't love God unless you hate the Devil. You can't love right unless you hate wrong. These namby-pamby preachers who never preach against anything don't love anything; theirs is a synthetic, superficial type of love. Theirs is a love that says to their young people, "I love you," but doesn't warn them against rock music. I say, that's not love at all.

The word *pastor* means "shepherd." A pastor is the shepherd of the flock. When God scolded his men who were not doing what they should, He likened them unto a shepherd who was not doing what he should do with his flock. God is using this figure of speech in Ezekiel 34, but God has His men in mind and the way His men handled the people in their flock. Ezekiel 34:19 says, "*And as for my flock* [the people of God], *they eat that which ye have trodden with your feet; and they drink that which ye have fouled with your feet.*" That word *fouled* means "you have caused it to stink." He is saying to the men of God, "You are like a shepherd who has a flock of sheep, and you are corrupting their food by walking on it with your dirty feet. You are also corrupting their water by putting your stinking feet in the water." God is likening that to God's men who dabble wrongly with the Word of God, our bread and water.

The whole issue of Ezekiel 34:19 is the Word of God. God is saying to His men, "Leave the Book alone; keep your stinking feet off my words." The Word of God is the drinking water for God's people and the cleanser for God's people. I'd like to say to the publishers who publish the *New International Version*—"Keep your stinking feet off the Word of God! That's my drinking water. Keep your stinking feet out of my drinking water." The RSV is dirty water. The ASV is dirty water. The NASV is dirty water. The NIV is dirty water. The *Reader's Digest Condensed Version* is dirty water. The *New King James Version* is dirty water. The publishers and translators have taken the pure Word of God and changed it for a dollar. So-called Christian colleges, take your stinking feet out of the Word of God! So-called Christian seminaries with your intelligentsia, keep your stinking feet out of my drinking water! Those theologians who say there is no perfect Bible in the English language, keep your stinking feet out of my drinking water! Self-styled Greek scholars, keep your stinking feet out of my drinking water!

Show me the pure water! I've got to have it! If it's the *American Standard Version*, stand up and say that the *American Standard Version* is flawless. I'd rather you say that than to say we have no pure water. If the NIV is flawless, stand up and say it! My Bible says that I have to have the pure Word of God.

Jesus said in Matthew 4:4, "...*Man shall not live by bread alone, but by every word that proceedeth out of the mouth of God.*" Jesus said, "*every word,*" not "every thought." God's people must have the pure Word of God.

John 15:7 says, "*If ye abide in me, and my words abide in you....*" Deuteronomy 4:10 says, "*...make them hear my words....*" John 14:23 says, "*...If a man love me, he will keep my words....*" If we are going to keep His words, we have to have His words—the pure, unadulterated words of Almighty God.

John 12:48 says, "*He that rejecteth me, and receiveth not my words....*" John 5:47 says, "*...how shall ye believe my words?*" Luke 1:20 says, "*...thou believest not my words....*" Mark 8:38 says, "*Whosoever therefore shall be ashamed of me and of my words...of him also shall the Son of man be ashamed, when he cometh in the glory of his Father with the holy angels.*" Mark 13:31 says, "*...my words shall not pass away.*" Luke 21:33 says, "*...my words shall not pass away.*" Isaiah 51:16 says, "*And I have put my words in thy mouth....*" Jeremiah 1:9 says, "*...I have put my words in thy mouth.*" Jeremiah 6:19 says, "*...I will bring evil upon this people,...because they have not hearkened unto my words....*" How can a person harken to His words if he does not have His words?

II Peter 3:2 says, "*That ye may be mindful of the words which were spoken before by the holy prophets....*" Revelation 1:3 says, "*...hear the words of this prophecy....*" Revelation 22:19 says, "*And if any man shall take away from the words of the book of this prophecy....*" Jeremiah 11:10 says, "*They are turned back to the iniquities of their forefathers, which refused to hear my words....*" Job 33:1 says, "*...hearken to all my words.*" Jeremiah 5:14 says, "*...I will make my words in thy mouth fire....*" Exodus 4:28 says, "*...all the words of the LORD....*" Exodus 24:4 says, "*...all the words of the LORD....*" Jeremiah 26:2 says, "*...speak all the words that I command thee....*" Psalm 107:11 says, "*Because they rebelled against the words of God....*" Jeremiah 26:2 says, "*...diminish not a word.*" Did you hear that, NIV folks? Don't take out a word! There has to be a book in this world some-where that contains all the words of God with not one word added and not one word taken away. I believe I hold it in my hand—the King James Bible. If you don't believe that, then show me what it is!

Psalm 119:103 says, "*How sweet are thy words unto my taste….*" Psalm 119:130 says, "*The entrance of thy words giveth light….*" Revelation 21:5 says, "*…these words are true….*" Jeremiah 25:30 says, "*…prophesy thou against them all these words.*" Proverbs 23:9 says, "*…a fool…will despise the wisdom of thy words.*" Jeremiah 3:12 says, "*Go and proclaim these words….*" Jeremiah 7:27 says, "*Therefore thou shalt speak all these words unto them….*" Jeremiah 26:15 says, "*…speak all these words….* " Jeremiah 51:61 says, "*…read all these words.*" Psalm 119:57 says, "*…I would keep thy words.*"I Thessalonians 4:18 says, "*Wherefore comfort one another with these words.*" Proverbs 23:8 says, "*…thy sweet words.*" II Samuel 7:28 says, "*…thou art that God, and thy words be true….*" Jeremiah 15:16 says, "*Thy words were found, and I did eat them….*" Psalm 55:21 says, "*…his words were softer than oil….*"

All these Scriptures tell us that we must have all the words of Almighty God. Now get your stinking feet out of my drinking water! Don't fool with my drinking water! Don't add to my drinking water! Don't take from my drinking water! Don't change my drinking water! Don't diminish my drinking water! Don't condense my drinking water! Don't make my drinking water easier to understand! Don't merchandise my drinking water!

Not one publisher in America is publishing all these Bibles because they want you to understand the Bible better or because they want to spread the Word of God. They are trying to make a buck! If the publishing houses wanted to make the Bible easier to understand, why do they copyright each of their Bibles? The King James Bible is not copyrighted. It's available to everybody. In God's name, quit peddling the Book of God for a dollar, and get back to getting out the literal, true words of God to a lost world.

Bible translators have messed up the virgin birth with their stinking feet. They have messed up the sinless life of Christ with their stinking feet. They have messed up the deity of Christ with their stinking feet. They have messed up the blood of Christ with your stinking feet. They have messed up the imminent return of Christ with your stinking feet.

We've got to get back to the Bible that built this nation. When America believed the King James Bible, we didn't have policemen in our schools. When our teachers in the public schools believed the King James Bible and started each morning with reading from the King James Bible, we didn't have the problems in our schools that we now have. America didn't have a bunch of drug problems when we believed the King James Bible.

Before a bunch of self-styled scholars thought they could change the King James Bible to make a buck, we had a nation worth something. We must return to the Bible that built this nation. We must get back to the Bible that built the great revival crusades that changed America. We've got to get back to the Bible that caused America to outlaw liquor at one time. We've got to get back to the Bible that caused America not to even know what marijuana was. We've got to get back to the Bible that made America an honest and decent nation—a nation that kept their vows when they stood at the altar, a nation that had integrity and paid their debts on the day they were due. This nation will not be saved until we get back to "...*every word that proceedeth out of the mouth of God.*" You so-called scholars are not fooling anybody; you are putting yourself above the God who built this country on this Book—the King James Bible.

Some will say that they want to make the Bible easier to understand. We fundamentalists have no problem understanding the King James Bible. Those who call us dumb have to have an easier Bible, and they are the so-called intellectuals. Maybe they should get an easier Bible. How dare you rise up against the God of the Bible and tell Him that He needs some help to give us a Bible! I have more respect for a state university professor who says that there is no Word of God than I have for a man who hides behind the sacred desk and changes God's blessed Book.

You say, I just don't believe the King James Bible is the Word of God. The Bible says, *"...Man shall not live by bread alone, but by every word that proceedeth out of the mouth of God."* If the King James Bible is not the Word of God, what is the Word of God? Find it! I can't live without it! I must have every word to live. I must have every word to get my prayers answered. I must have every word to receive Christ. I must have every word to keep Him from being ashamed of me. I must have every word to prevent evil from coming upon me. I must have every word to be on fire for God. I must have every word if I speak God's message. I have to have every word to love Him. I have to have every word not to reject Him. I have to have every word to meditate. I have to have every word to avoid the plagues of God. I have to have every word to have an eternal Bible. I have to have every word to be comforted. I have to have every word to have wisdom. I have to have every word to have the truth and gain light. I have to have every word to preach. Quick! Show me the real words!

There must be a perfect Bible somewhere. Which one is it? If you believe it is the ASV or the NASV, speak up. If you believe it is the NIV, speak up. If you believe it is the *Reader's Digest Condensed Version*, speak up. If we must have a Bible that contains *"every word that proceedeth out of the mouth of God,"* that means that only one is right. You say, "I have several versions, and each version sheds some light on the others." Why don't you get saved, and the Holy Spirit will shed the light on the King James Bible. I am as mad as a hornet because the translators and publishers are putting their stinking feet in my drinking water.

Most fundamentalists will agree that the King James Bible contains the very words of God; yet, many of us are dehydrated. We believe the King James Bible, but we don't read it. How much have you read this week? We believe the Bible, but we don't learn it. We believe the Bible, but we don't meditate upon it. How long do you spend each week meditating upon the Bible? Psalm 1:1, 2, *"Blessed is the man that walketh not in the counsel of the ungodly, nor standeth in the way of sinners, nor sitteth in the seat of the scornful. But his delight is in the law of the LORD; and in his law doth he meditate day and night."* Yes, you believe it, but how much have you memorized? If someone put a gun to your head and said, "Quote ten verses or I'll pull the trigger," would you be in Heaven soon? Would you have to say *"Jesus wept"* ten times? We believe the King James Bible from cover to cover, but many of us never open the cover. If the King James Bible is the Word of God preserved by God Almighty, then God help us to get in it and read it and study it.

God gave us several commands concerning God's Word:
- Psalm 119:1—I'm to walk in it.
- Psalm 119:2—I am to keep it.
- Psalm 119:6—I am to respect it.
- Psalm 119:7—I am to learn it.
- Psalm 119:9—I am to take heed to it.
- Psalm 119:10—I am not to wander from it.
- Psalm 119:11—I am to hide it in my heart.
- Psalm 119:13—I am supposed to declare it.
- Psalm 119:14—I am to rejoice in it.
- Psalm 119:15—I am to meditate on the Word of God.
- Psalm 119:16—I am to delight in it.
- Psalm 119:20—I am to long for it.
- Psalm 119:24—I am to seek counsel from the Bible.

- Psalm 119:26—I am to learn the Word of God.
- Psalm 119:27—I am to understand it.
- Psalm 119:30—I am to choose the Word of God.
- Psalm 119:31—I am to stand with the Word of God.
- Psalm 119:32—I am to run the way of the Word of God.
- Psalm 119:34—I am to observe with my whole heart the Word of God.
- Psalm 119:35—I am to go in the path of the Word of God.
- Psalm 119:36—I am to incline my heart toward the Word of God.
- Psalm 119:42—I am to trust in the Word of God.
- Psalm 119:43—I am to hope in the Word of God.
- Psalm 119:46—I am to speak the Word of God.
- Psalm 119:48—I am to lift up my hands to the Word of God.
- Psalm 119:49—I am to remember the Word of God.
- Psalm 119:50—I am to be quickened by the Word of God.
- Psalm 119:51—I am not to decline from the Word of God.
- Psalm 119:54—I am to sing the Word of God.
- Psalm 119:59—I am to think on the Word of God.
- Psalm 119:61—I am not to forget the Word of God.
- Psalm 119:66—I am to believe all of the Word of God.
- Psalm 119:80—I am not to be ashamed of the Word of God.

How can we obey all the commands given to us concerning the words of God if we don't have the perfect words of God?

Those of you who don't believe the King James Bible is the perfect Word of God, don't pollute my water with your stinking thought inspiration. Don't come to me with your "only the original is inspired." Don't come to me with your stinking versions! Get your dirty feet out of my drinking water. Don't come to me with your stinking *Amplified Bible* or your stinking *Vernacular Bible*. Don't come to me with your stinking works salvation. Don't come to me with your stinking confession to the priest. Don't come to me with your stinking lordship salvation. Get your stinking feet out of my drinking water.

Don't come to me with your stinking invisible church doctrine. Don't come to me with your stinking bloodless mercy seat. Don't come to me with your stinking falling from grace. Don't come to me with your stinking baptismal regeneration. Don't come to me with your stinking sacramental salvation. Don't come to me with your stinking confirmation salvation. Don't come to me with your stinking life-style evangelism. Don't come to me with your stinking mid-tribulation rapture. Don't come to me with your stinking NIV Bible. Don't come to me with your stinking RSV or ASV or NASV or your New King James or your New Scofield. Get your stinking feet out of my drinking water!

Let us, as fundamentalists, stand and hold our shoulders back and our chests out and say, "We proudly believe the King James Bible contains the preserved words of God Almighty." While we hold the Bible high, let's not keep it shut. Let's open it, and live in it, and study it, and learn it, and teach it, and memorize it.

Chapter Fourteen

Not One Word Has Failed, Nor Has One Tittle Passed Away

I Kings 8:54-61 says, "And it was so, that when Solomon had made an end of praying all this prayer and supplication unto the LORD, he arose from before the altar of the LORD, from kneeling on his knees with his hands spread up to heaven. And he stood, and blessed all the congregation of Israel with a loud voice, saying, Blessed be the LORD, that hath given rest unto his people Israel, according to all that he promised: there hath not failed one word of all his good promise, which he promised by the hand of Moses his servant. The LORD our God be with us, as he was with our fathers: let him not leave us, nor forsake us: That he may incline our hearts unto him, to walk in all his ways, and to keep his commandments, and his statutes, and his judgments, which he commanded our fathers. And let these my words, wherewith I have made supplication before the LORD, be nigh unto the LORD our God day and night, that he maintain the cause of his servant, and the cause of his people Israel at all times, as the matter shall require: That all the people of the earth may know that the LORD is God, and that there is none else. Let your heart therefore be perfect with the LORD our God, to walk in his statutes, and to keep his commandments, as at this day."

Luke 16:17 says, "And it is easier for heaven and earth to pass, than one tittle of the law to fail."

A preacher once asked me, "You don't believe in verbal inspiration, do you?"

I said, "I believe in tittle inspiration."

What was a tittle as mentioned in the Bible? A "tittle" is similar to an accent mark which is used to emphasize a syllable. God is saying, "Not one word, not one accent mark, not one punctuation mark shall pass away."

I Kings 8:56 says, *"Blessed be the LORD, that hath given rest unto his people Israel, according to all that he promised: there hath not failed one word of all his good promise, which he promised by the hand of Moses his servant."*

This passage refers to the Pentateuch, the first five books of the Bible. The verse was not written two weeks after the Pentateuch was written. It was probably written over 2,000 years after the Pentateuch was written. Miraculously, for nearly 2,500 years, God preserved His Word exactly as He gave it to Moses.

During the first three centuries after Christ, the Roman Empire tried to stamp out the Word of God. While the Roman Empire is buried in the cemetery of kingdom failures, the Bible lives on. In the eighth century, as Mohammedanism tried to exterminate the Bible, the false prophet only inspired the Bible to be more widespread to the rest of the world. Nero ordered the Bible's destruction; yet, Nero is in Hell while the Bible lives on. Hitler said he would destroy the Bible; Hitler is dead and the Bible lives on. Stalin said that he would trample God's Word. Stalin's feet lie in the dust; yet the Bible is trampling on, and trampling its enemies. Lenin said that the Bible would die in his day; Lenin died, and the Bible still lives. Thomas Paine said that the Bible would cease to be printed in his lifetime. Yet, after Paine died, the very printing presses on which he printed his garbage were used to print more Bibles. Voltaire tried to destroy it. Voltaire is dead and in Hell; yet, the Bible lives on. Khrushchev tried to destroy it. Khrushchev is dead, and the Bible lives on. Brezhnev tried to destroy it. Brezhnev is dead, and the Bible lives on. Mussolini tried to destroy it in Italy. Mussolini is dead, and the Bible lives on. Nebuchadnezzar tried to destroy the Word of God. Although Nebuchadnezzar has been dead for several thousand years, the Bible still lives on. Today secular universities have tried to destroy the Bible, but when these so-called professors are burning in Hell, the Bible will still live on.

Publishers have tried to destroy the Bible by publishing so-called new Bibles, but the old King James Bible is healthier today than it ever has been. Seminaries, so-called Christian colleges, and Bible institutes have tried to pervert, add to, take away, change, and destroy the Bible; yet, the Bible lives on.

The Bible is the only eternal Book in the entire world. There never was a time when the Bible did not exist, just like there never was a time when Jesus did not exist. John, the beloved said, *"In the beginning was the Word, and the Word was with God, and the Word was God. The same was in the beginning with God."* There never was a time when there was no Heavenly Father; there never was a time when there was no Holy Spirit; and there never was a time when God's eternal Book did not exist. It always has been. Matthew 24:35 says, *"Heaven and earth shall pass away, but my words shall not pass away."*

I Peter 1:23 says, *"...the word of God, which liveth and abideth for ever."* Mark 13:31 says, *"Heaven and earth shall pass away: but my words shall not pass away."* I Peter 1:25 says, *"But the word of the LORD endureth for ever...."* Isaiah 40:8 says, *"The grass withereth, the flower fadeth: but the word of our God shall stand for ever."* Matthew 5:18, *"...One jot or one tittle shall in no wise pass from the law...."* Luke 21:33 says, *"...my words shall not pass away."*

What am I saying? I'm saying that the Bible is the only writing in the whole world that will endure forever. When the kingdoms of this earth have become history, the Bible will still linger. When the dictators of this world have laughed at it for the last time, the Bible will still linger. When the mountains have been leveled and the valleys have been raised, when kingdoms have crumbled and heaven and earth have passed away, the Bible shall live forever.

Yet, in the average Christian's home, the Bible remains closed while they watch talk shows or the prime-time television programs. Talk shows will pass away. Prime-time television will pass away. Soap operas will pass away. Newspapers will pass away. Magazines will pass away. The entertainment industry and the media will all pass away, but the Bible will never pass away!

The Hammond *Times* will pass away. There will be no vending machines in Heaven where you can pick up a Hammond *Times* on the way home from work. The *Tribune* will not be delivered to your doorstep. There will be no *Ladies' Home Journal*. There will be no *Sports' Illustrated*. There will be no newsstands. There will be no *Wall Street Journal, Reader's Digest, National Geographic, Newsweek, U. S. News and World Report, Woman's Home Companion, Vogue, New York Times, Atlanta Constitution, Dallas Morning News, U.S.A. Today, Playboy, Penthouse, Los Angeles Times, Minneapolis Star, St. Louis Globe Democrat, San Francisco Examiner, Ft. Worth Star Telegram, Detroit News, Detroit Free Press, Houston Chronicle, New Orleans Picayune, Miami Herald, Corpus Christi Caller Times, Charlotte Observer, Philadelphia Enquirer, Atlanta Journal, Akron Journal, Indianapolis Star, Chicago Daily Herald,* or *Des Moines Register.* However, the Bible will abide forever and ever and ever and ever.

No, we won't be able to pick up the *U.S.A. Today* newspaper in Heaven. Instead, we can read the *Galveston Genesis,* and the *El Paso Exodus,* and the *Los Angeles Leviticus,* and the *New Orleans Numbers,* and the *Dallas Deuteronomy,* and the

Jacksonville Joshua, and the *Jackson Judges*, and the *Rochester Ruth*, and the *San Antonio Samuel*, and the *Kansas City Kings*, and the *Chicago Chronicles*, and the *Emporia Ezra*, and the *New York Nehemiah*, and the *Evansville Esther*, and the *Jamestown Job*, and the *Pittsburgh Psalms*, and the *Philadelphia Proverbs*, and the *Enterprise Ecclesiastes*, and the *San Francisco Song of Solomon*, and the *Iron Mountain Isaiah*, and the *Jonesboro Jeremiah*, and the *Las Vegas Lamentations*, and the *Escondido Ezekiel*, and the *Detroit Daniel*, and the *Houston Hosea*, and the *Minneapolis Minor Prophets*, and the *Mobile Matthew*, and the *Manchester Mark*, and the *Los Alamos Luke*, and the *Jeffersonville John*, and the *Atlanta Acts*, and the *Rockport Romans*, and the *Cincinnati Corinthians*, and the *Galena Galatians*, and the *Eureka Ephesians*, and the *Pinellas Park Philippians*, and the *Cleveland Colossians*, and the *Tulsa Thessalonians*, and the *Tampa Timothy*, and the *Toledo Titus*, and the *Honolulu Hebrews*, and the *Johnsonville James*, and the *Port Arthur Peter*, and the *Judson John*, and *Junction City Jude*, and the *Rock Island Revelation*. Only the Bible will be available in the dispensers in Heaven!

Some Christians may not enjoy Heaven. I mean that. They will be bored to death. Those who don't enjoy church here on earth won't enjoy Heaven at all. Those who don't enjoy the songs of God here won't enjoy the songs of God there. Those who don't enjoy this eternal Book now will not enjoy the Bible when they get to Heaven.

We'll spend eternity listening to Moses teach a course on the Pentateuch, Paul teaching the Epistles, David teaching the Psalms, Solomon teaching the Proverbs, John teaching the four Gospels and I, II, and III John, Isaiah teaching the Major Prophets, Daniel teaching prophecy, Hosea teaching the Minor Prophets, Job teaching patience, Paul teaching church planting, David teaching music, and Philip teaching soul winning.

Look What God Has Done with His Word!

By His Word, He created the earth. By His Word, He raised the Adirondack Mountains. By His Word, He lifted the Rockies. By His Word, He elevated the Alps. By His Word, He carved the gorges. By His Word, He painted the desert. By His Word, He wiggled the mighty Amazon. By His Word, He whittled the Mississippi. By His Word, He filled the oceans. By His Word, He poured the lakes. By His Word, He lowered the valleys. By His Word, He leveled the plains. By His Word, He rounded the hills. By His Word, He chiseled Gibraltar. By His Word, islands were resurrected from watery graves. By His Word, He formed the billowy clouds. By His Word, He scented the gardenia. By His Word, He painted the rose. By His Word, He arranged the daffodil. By His Word, He formed Diamond Head, the Grand Canyon, and the Carlsbad Caverns. All were created by the Word of God! You have a copy of it. In God's name, read it! Read it! Read it!

Everything God has ever done, He has done with His Word. In the creation story, ten times the Bible says, "*And God said.*" Genesis 1:3 says, "*And God said, Let there be light: and there was light.*" Everything that God ever created, He created by His Word.

By His Word, Jesus stilled the stormy winds. By His Word, He calmed the nervous seas. By His Word, He gave sight to blind Bartimaeus. By His Word, He raised Lazarus from an angry grave. By His Word, He directed a fish to swallow a coin. By His Word, He called that fish to Himself. By His Word, that fish vomited the coin so Jesus could pay His taxes. By His Word, He healed the crippled at Bethesda. By His Word, He expelled demons. By His Word, He fed 5,000 people with five loaves and two fishes. By His Word, He turned the water into wine. By His Word, He commanded devils to resign. By His Word, He roto-rootered deaf ears. By His Word, He resisted

Satan's temptation. By His Word, He reinforced crippled legs. By His Word, He gave intelligence to dumb tongues. By His Word, He postponed a funeral during its processional. By His Word, He cast demons into hogs and caused the hogs to plunge to their deaths into the water.

God speaks, and the sun rises and sets. God speaks, and the moon changes its shape. He speaks, and the rain falls. He speaks, and snow tiptoes to the earth. He speaks, and lightning gives its great fireworks demonstration while thunder applauds its performance.

Everything that God has ever done, He has done through the Bible. Yet, families try to build a home without the Bible. Couples try to build a marriage without the Bible. Christians try to build a life without the Bible. New evangelicals try to build churches without the Bible.

By His Word, God laid the foundations of the earth. By His Word, He laid the earth's cornerstone. By His Word, He drops the morning dew. By His Word, He sends the hoary frost from Heaven. By His Word, the raven is sent as lunch. By His Word, He painted the wings of the peacock. By His Word, He commands the eagle to rev its motors for a take off and landing. By His Word, He shakes the earth into a quake. Even when Jesus comes again, He will conquer the Antichrist by the spirit of His mouth and the brightness of His coming.

By His Word, Jesus will win the Battle of Armageddon. Before the Second Coming of Christ, Russia will invade Palestine because of the riches in the Dead Sea. Libya, Eastern Germany, Turkey, Iran, and other nations will join Russia in her march on little Israel. America will rise in defense of Israel. The western powers, led by the United States of America, will fight Russia on the mountains of Israel. The United States and her allies will be winning the battle, and Russia will seek help from the eastern nations. The Euphrates River will be dried, allowing China and Japan to attack Israel from the east. The western powers will win that battle, and a man called the Antichrist will rise up to be dictator of all the earth. The Antichrist will look toward the south and say, "I've conquered the south." He will look toward the east and say, "I've conquered the east." He will look toward the west and say, "I've conquered the west." He will look toward the north and say, "I've conquered the north." But, there's one place he won't look: toward the sky. The sky will open, and Jesus Himself, with all the holy angels and saints of God will descend on white horses. Will Jesus destroy the forces of the Antichrist with bombs and airplanes and mortars and guns and other weapons? No! He will speak, and the battle will be won!

Jesus was tempted by Satan to turn the stones into bread. He resisted the Devil by saying. "*It is written, Man shall not live by bread alone, but by every word that proceedeth out of the mouth of God.*" The Devil came another time and tempted Jesus again by taking Him up on the pinnacle of the temple, and saying, "Jump off, and people will see that you are God."

Jesus once again was tempted, but resisted the Devil by saying a second time, "*It is written.*" Then the Devil took Him and showed Him the kingdoms of the earth, and said, "These are my kingdoms. I'm the god of this world. Bow down and worship me, and I'll give you all these kingdoms."

Jesus said for the third time, "*It is written.*" If the Son of God Himself fought the temptations of Satan with the Word, "*It is written,*" how can Christians think they are going to get by without the Word of God?

By His Word, God files the flight plan for every bird and determines when or where he falls or lands. By His Word, He charts the watery journey of every fish that swims. By His Word, He leads the instinct of every beast in the field. By His Word, He chose to give us the mighty lion. By His Word, he chose to amuse us with the funny hippo, to startle us with the strange giraffe, and to feed us with the grazing cattle. By His

Word, He gave us beans and spinach and cauliflower and squash and carrots and peas and broccoli and fried okra and oranges and apples and bananas and pears and watermelon.

By His Word, He created everything. On the first day of creation, God divided light from darkness by His Word. On the second day, He divided the waters above from the waters beneath by His Word. On the third day, plant life appeared by His Word. On the fourth day, sun, moon, and stars were made visible by His Word. On the fifth day, He created the beast of the field by His Word. On the sixth day, He created man and woman by His Word. Everything was created by the ever-living, never-dying, never-extinguished Word of God!

Psalm 119:11 says His Word keeps us from sin. Psalm 119:28 says His Word keeps us strong. John 15:7 says His Word is the key to answered prayer. I Peter 2:2 says His Word helps us to grow in grace. II Peter 1:4 says His Word makes us partakers of His divine nature. Acts 20:32 says His Word builds us up. II Timothy 3:16 says His Word reproves, corrects, and instructs. Hebrews 4:12 says His Word gives us proper thoughts and motives. Proverbs 30:5 says His Word shields us. Joshua 1:8 says His Word makes us prosperous and successful. Psalm 119:165 says His Word keeps us from being offended. Luke 1:79 says His Word gives us peace. John 8:32 says His Word gives us freedom. Psalm 119:105 says His Word is a lamp to our feet and a light unto our path. Proverbs 4:22 says His Word gives us health. One Book—the Bible!

It is the Book that remains closed while Christians watch television. It is the Book that is read less than the daily newspaper. The Bible is a combination and a compilation. It will do more good than health clubs plus motivational books plus success seminars plus Alcoholics Anonymous plus the psychologists and psychiatrists plus possibility thinking plus the Promise Keepers—this one Book!

The Bible remains closed and unread by many Christians.

A marriage cannot be built without the Word of God. A home cannot be built without the Word of God. A public school cannot be built by kicking out the Word of God. A business cannot be built without the Word of God. A church cannot be built without the Word of God. A college cannot be built without the Word of God. And we will not build a great nation without the Word of God.

Charismatic, you can have your word of knowledge; I'll take the Word of God. You can have your charismatic messages that supposedly come from Heaven; I'll take the Book that came from Heaven and has been preserved word for word all these years. You can have your visions; give me the Word of God. You can have your possibility thinking; give me the Word of God. You can have your *American Standard Version*; give me the Word of God. You can have your *New American Standard Version*; give me the Word of God. You can have your *New International Version*; give me the Old King James preserved Word of God. You can have your *New King James Version*; give me the Word of God. You can have your *Reader's Digest Condensed Version*; give me the Word of God. You can have your *New Scofield Version*; give me the Word of God. You can have your *Philip's Translation*; give me the Word of God. You can have your *Goodspeed Translation*; give me the Word of God. You can have your *Amplified New Testament*; give me the Word of God. You can have your Moffatt's Bible; give me the Word of God. You can have the Book of Mormon; give me the Word of God. You can have the *Koran*; just give me God's eternal words!

Give me that indestructible, all-powerful, eternal, unconquerable, inexhaustible, verbally inspired Word of God. Not one word has failed, and not even one tittle or accent shall pass away.

Conclusion

I was invited to be on the overview committee of the *New King James Version*. Of course, I turned it down. By mistake, I got into one of that committee's meetings, thinking it was another meeting. The men at that table were a hall of fame; famous men that most fundamentalists would love to know.

The chairman of the overview committee stood up, called the meeting to order, and they all started working. On one side of the table were seminary professors doing the research for the *New King James Version*. Not wanting to be rude by walking out, I just sat there for over an hour and listened as they all talked.

Finally, the chairman looked at me and said, "Dr. Hyles, you haven't said anything yet. How do you feel about the progress we've made thus far on the *New King James Bible?*"

I said, "I must tell you. I didn't want to say it out loud, but I must tell you. I am not for what is going on. I have the only Bible I want, and I don't need anything else."

I pointed to those seminary professors, with their so-called doctorate degrees that they gave each other, and I said, "You fellows ought to get out of here, get the King James Bible you've got and go soul winning. Preach some old-fashioned revival campaigns, and get a bunch of people out of Hell!

Spend your time doing that, and when you stand before God, you'll be more pleasing to Him than if you publish a Bible we don't need!"